DESIGN THINKING

DESIGN THINKING

a guide to innovation

FRED ESTES

TWENTY-FIRST CENTURY BOOKS / MINNEAPOLIS

For David Kelley and Kim Saxe, who mentored me and always inspire me.

Twenty-First Century Books™
An imprint of Lerner Publishing Group, Inc.
241 First Avenue North
Minneapolis, MN 55401 USA

For reading levels and more information, look up this title at www.lernerbooks.com.

Main body text set in Adobe Garamond Pro.
Typeface provided by Adobe Systems.

Library of Congress Cataloging-in-Publication Data

Names: Estes, Fred, 1950– author.
Title: Design thinking : a guide to innovation / Fred Estes.
Description: Minneapolis : Twenty-First Century Books, [2025] | Includes bibliographical references and index. | Audience: Ages 12–18 | Audience: Grades 7–9 | Summary: "Design Thinking by Fred Estes provides a simple, clear approach to the design thinking process. The easy-to-follow guide explains everything essential to your design-thinking projects focused on solving human-centered, social issues to effect change and to create a more equitable world"— Provided by publisher.
Identifiers: LCCN 2023052906 (print) | LCCN 2023052907 (ebook) | ISBN 9798765608005 (library binding) | ISBN 9798765638866 (epub)
Subjects: LCSH: Industrial design—Philosophy.
Classification: LCC TS171.4 .E86 2025 (print) | LCC TS171.4 (ebook) | DDC 670—dc23/eng/20240207

LC record available at https://lccn.loc.gov/2023052906
LC ebook record available at https://lccn.loc.gov/2023052907

Manufactured in the United States of America
3-1014407-51436-4/23/2026

CONTENTS

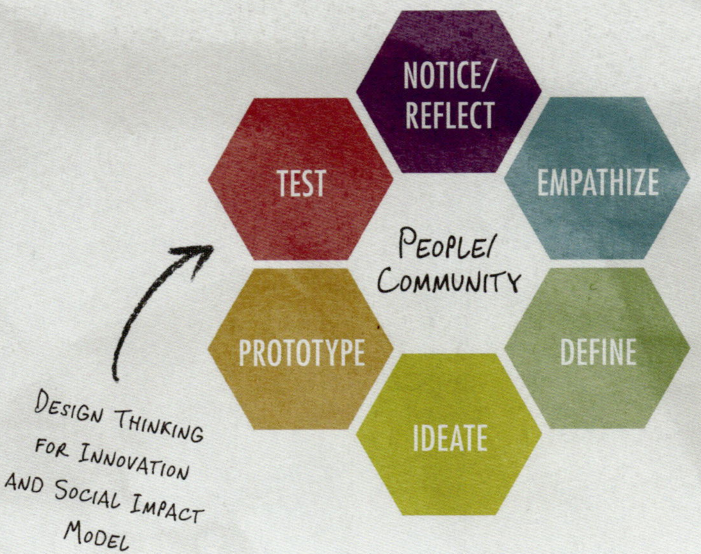

INTRODUCTION

Design Thinking for Innovation and Social Impact

Many people say that kids are the future, but we are here *now*, and we can make a difference.

—GITANJALI RAO, ELEVEN, IN 2017

The Stria Story

Imagine if you couldn't tell whether you were walking in a straight line or not because you weren't able to see. How would you navigate a street busy with traffic? This is a very common and serious problem for the blind community.

"We think we're going on a straight path and the next thing we know we're in the street facing oncoming traffic." Javier, blinded in an accident, is talking about "veering," the natural tendency to turn from a straight path without visual cues. He recalls one particular episode

A teacher models the Stria band, designed to help blind people from veering off course while walking.

of veering disorientation. "I was walking down the street and made a left without even realizing it. The next thing I know, I'm walking in between cars on the street."

A team of high school sophomores enrolled in a design thinking class wanted to find out if design thinking could help people like Javier. Their inspirational teacher, Connie Liu, created this elective class focused on designing for social good at the Nueva School in San Mateo, California.

After considering a range of options, this team knew they wanted to work on a project to help the blind community. Over six million people are legally blind in the US, and many more have limited vision. How, they wondered, could they have an impact? Nolyn, one of the students working on the project, said, "Blindness is such a large issue and the idea that a few high schoolers can take on such a big problem affecting so many people drew me to the project."

In addition to online research, they began with field trips to centers for the blind to help them empathize with the needs of people like Javier. At such places as the Vista Center for the Blind and Visually Impaired and LightHouse for the Blind and Visually Impaired, they interviewed people in the community and the professional staff to learn more about blindness. "I didn't know much about blindness until visiting the Vista Center," said Maya, another team member. "After telling them about our project, they were just so welcoming. It was super humbling."

Having spent some time learning about types of challenges that exist in the community, the team decided to tackle the problem of veering and started their background research. They concluded that a wearable device could be a significant improvement over the existing solutions. They met Javier, who agreed to partner with them on this project.

The group wanted to answer the question: How could people know when they veer? After brainstorming many possible solutions, they defined their idea to design a smart band that would give feedback to the walker using microelectronics. One challenge they faced was that many on the team were new to microelectronics and did not know microcontroller code. With characteristic enthusiasm and hard work, they learned about electricity, microelectronics, and coding microcontrollers as they built prototypes of the band. Driven to make a difference, they persevered through many failures to test and refine their design.

The team named their smart band Stria. The belt would have small vibrating motors on each side of the walker's waist. Sensors would indicate when a person was veering in one direction and then signal the motor on that side to vibrate, alerting the walker to make a slight turn in the opposite direction. The vibrations would continue to provide feedback until the walker was back on course. This technology is especially useful in noisy and crowded public places where navigation by sound is not safe.

This all sounded good, but would it work in practice? To test their idea, the team made simple belts out of cardboard and attached hand-operated buzzers. First on team members and then with Javier, they tested these prototypes to see if the buzzing sensation worked. After many trials and lots of input from Javier, they had a basic design.

Finding Your Design Project

How do you find a design project to work on if you are not part of a design thinking program at school or through a community center?

- **Community needs survey.** Talk to friends and neighbors, businesses, and community leaders to identify challenges they face. Every community has issues that need fixing.
- **Local nonprofits and organizations.** Reach out to local nonprofit organizations, community centers, or charities that often lack the staff or time to address challenges they're facing and would likely appreciate your creative thinking.
- **Local government.** Many local governments have challenges they're trying to address, from waste management to community engagement. Attend town hall meetings or reach out directly to identify areas where you might be able to help.
- **Community events.** Organize or participate in local hackathons, brainstorming sessions, or community workshops. The goal of these events is often to solve local challenges, and they are a great place to find a project and meet like-minded individuals.
- **Look around you.** Sometimes, the best design challenges are the ones you face in your daily life. Is there a local park that's underutilized? A traffic problem in your neighborhood? Start with what you know and experience every day.
- **Start small.** If you're new to design thinking, it's OK to start with a small, personal project. For instance, redesigning a process in your home or helping a family member with a challenge can be a good starting point.

You can probably think of many other ideas using these starting points. While the end solution is important, the process of design thinking—noticing and reflecting, empathizing, defining, ideating, prototyping, and testing—is where the real learning and innovation happens. Regardless of the scale of the project, there's always something valuable to gain from the process.

Javier demonstrates using the Stria band while walking.

When completed, the Stria band operated well and allowed blind people to walk the streets more safely. Javier thinks of it as a lifesaver and says the Stria team impressed him, remarking, "Wow, [they] really want to help us." Though the team won awards and attracted media attention, making life safer for Javier and the blind community was their greatest reward.

You can develop innovative solutions to assist others too. With design thinking skills, you can tackle problems like Javier's, making someone's burden a bit lighter and someone's world a bit better.

What Is Design Thinking?

Design thinking is a systematic approach to creative problem-solving, centering on the needs of people and our global community. The innovation and social impact method in this book focuses on empathy, collaboration, and continual learning. Applying these practices helps designers craft innovative, sustainable, and equitable solutions.

Sustainable solutions meet the current needs of our communities while maintaining the long-term health of our environment. Equitable solutions focus on fairness by providing people with the resources they need to succeed. Since people have different needs and circumstances, design thinking recognizes the necessity to adapt and individualize solutions.

Designing for social impact seeks answers for unsolved problems, including those problems creating social barriers and biases that are part of a system. These solutions for unmet needs aim to improve lives while supporting the goals of social justice.

This social impact design strategy begins with reflecting on your own values and motivations to avoid a "rescuer" mentality. Almost nothing undermines a true partnership more quickly. Engage genuinely with your partners in the community to collaborate on problem-solving. Develop a deep understanding of their needs and those of the community by engaging in authentic dialogue.

While this book is not primarily about applying design thinking to social justice issues—although that would be an important book someone should write—it is about keeping equity and social justice concerns as an essential part of the design thinking process.

Building on this foundation, you can work together to solve problems faced by your partners while considering the social good of the entire community.

The **Design Thinking for Innovation and Social Impact** (DTISI) process model extends the famous design thinking model originated by IDEO and the Stanford d.school. That approach shifted the primary focus of design to the needs of people, rather than focusing on purely technical efficiency as many traditional engineering methods did. The aim of DTISI is to capture the core of IDEO/d.school design thinking while enriching it with a focus on social equity and community engagement.

The Design Thinking for Innovation and Social Impact model integrates the Notice/Reflect elements from the National Equity Project's Equity-Centered Design model. This emphasizes the importance of self-awareness and contextual understanding. Both of these ideas are crucial when designing solutions that are not only innovative but also socially responsible.

In addition to the models mentioned above, there are a variety of design thinking approaches that adapt the core principles for different purposes and challenges. Here are some that have influenced the Design Thinking for Innovation and Social Impact model:

- **Double Diamond.** The British Design Council's model maps the design process through four phases of divergent and convergent thinking: Discover, Define, Develop, and Deliver.
- **IDEO's Simplified Design Thinking Framework.** IDEO, the renowned design and consulting firm, uses a three-stage process: Inspire, Ideate, and Implement.
- **LUMA Institute's System of Innovation.** The LUMA Institute uses a human-centered approach organized around three key areas: Looking, Understanding, and Making.
- **Head, Heart, and Hand Model.** This model by the American Institute of Graphic Arts focuses on empathy, creativity, and action. It encourages designers to engage emotionally, think creatively, and execute effectively.
- **Service Design Thinking.** Focused on service improvements, this model combines empathy, creativity, and practicality to create services that truly meet user needs.
- **Circular Design.** Circular design aligns with the principles of environmental stewardship, sustainability, and social responsibility. By adopting circular practices, we can create a more sustainable future for people, business, and nature.

While this medley of models might seem confusing, most of them, including Design Thinking for Innovation and Social Impact, share some common elements:

1. **START BY UNDERSTANDING PEOPLE**
   Begin by really getting to know and empathizing with the people you're designing for. Find out what they need and want to create solutions that truly help them, as well as benefit businesses and the whole community.
2. **LOOK AT THE PROBLEM FROM ALL ANGLES**
   Take your time to understand the challenge before trying to solve it. Look at it from different viewpoints to really grasp what's going on.
3. **THINK BROADLY AT FIRST**
   Start by unleashing your creative imagination and gathering lots of different ideas and insights. Encourage everyone to come up with creative solutions without worrying about being right or wrong.
4. **NARROW YOUR FOCUS LATER**
   After you have a list of ideas, start to narrow them down. Sort through what you've gathered, combine the best parts of different ideas, and start to shape them into more complete solutions.
5. **MAKE MODELS AND TRY THEM OUT**
   Build simple prototype versions of your solutions and see how they work. Try them out, find out what's not quite right, and make improvements.
6. **KEEP IMPROVING BY ITERATING**
   Continue reviewing and refining your solutions. As you learn more, go back and think through the challenge again. Refine your solution based on what you've learned.

Each of the following chapters explains one phase in the process model with clear, sequential instructions. Every chapter will feature a diagram of the Design Thinking for Innovation and Social Impact model that provides a visual cue and displays your progress. The true stories of real student teams and their projects provide context and depth. You will meet Kate, Sam, Preston, and Eliot of Team Syphon in the Empathize chapter; Lilli and Avery of Team Squggle in the Define chapter; and Dev and Mark of Team Alertra in the Ideate chapter.

Helpful tips appear in sidebars, and diagrams further clarify points. Each chapter ends with reflection questions to help you connect the content to your own experience and a completion checklist to help you track your project.

At the end of the book, the Going Further section provides resources to learn more about specific design thinking techniques. A glossary has terms that may be unfamiliar.

Author's Notes on Language and Usage

Clear writing and respectful language should always go together. This value aligns well with the principles of empathy and consideration that are central to design thinking and the social impact theme of this book.

- I use aliases for the names of people mentioned in this book unless I have their written permission.
- When referring to a person whose pronouns I do not know, I will use *they*, *them*, or *theirs*.
- Project Invent refers to the people their student teams design for as "community partners," rather than "users." I like this term much better and use it throughout this book.
- I aim for respectful, non-stigmatizing language when referring to people in different communities. Language, however, is ever changing. I use the identity-first convention (e.g., "blind people" rather than "people who are blind"), which follows current community preferences.
- This book is intended for both individual designers and multi-person design teams, and all references to "you and your team" should be read as "you, or you and your team." As a reader and a writer, I find "and/or" awkward.
- Design thinkers make solutions for their community partners that may either be physical devices, such as a waistband with sensors, or a process innovation, such as creating an after-school program. All references to "solutions," "inventions," "creations," or similar terms are intended for both devices and processes.

Project Invent

The Design Thinking Institute was started as a summer program by David Kelley and Kim Saxe at the Nueva School. One very important spin-off from the Design Thinking Institute is Project Invent. Connie Liu, one of the Nueva teachers with whom I taught in the Design Thinking Institute, founded Project Invent to help bring design thinking to even more students and teachers. This nonprofit organization empowers students to invent technologies for social good.

Project Invent pairs community members with teams of student inventors to design creative solutions for personal and local problems. Teams Syphon, Squggle, and Alertra, featured in this book, are Project Invent teams from around the United States. More information about Project Invent and contact information is in the Going Further section of this book.

How to Use This Book

Use this book as a flexible guide for you, your team, and your community partners. You might read it straight through and then go back to chapters or resources you want to revisit, or you may jump directly to chapters or resources you want to focus on now.

This book is not a rigid recipe to be followed to the letter. Go ahead and adapt it for your needs. Adjust the recommendations and steps to fit your community situation. While I give tips on how to solve common problems, every real-life situation is different. Be creative and improvise. Use design thinking to jump-start your ideas to solve problems in your community and in the world.

Having the right mindset–your mental attitude–determines how we approach problems and work toward solutions. In design thinking, certain attitudes help us think, feel, and act effectively during projects. Here are the key mindsets for successful design thinking:

1. **BE EMPATHETIC**
   Try to truly understand people by seeing things from their perspective. This means considering the needs and motivations of everyone in the community.
2. **BE COLLABORATIVE**
   Teamwork is key to success. Combining the strengths and ideas of everyone on the team usually leads to better outcomes than working alone.
3. **STAY OPTIMISTIC**
   Keep a positive mental attitude. We have the power to create meaningful change, starting with small steps and focused efforts, regardless of the scale of the challenge or the limitations of resources.
4. **EMBRACE UNCERTAINTY**
   Be open to complex and unclear situations. Avoid seeking certainty or perfection at the start. This allows for the risk-taking that is essential for innovative solutions. Design thinking encourages trying things out and learning as you go.
5. **BE CURIOUS**
   Always be ready to explore new ideas and understand that your viewpoint isn't the only one.
6. **THINK DIFFERENT**
   Don't accept problems as they appear. Challenge your initial assumptions. Recognize that looking for patterns can sometimes lead us to form limiting stereotypes. Design thinking encourages breaking past these old patterns to see problems in a new light.
7. **VALUE DIFFERENT PERSPECTIVES**
   Seek to work with people from various cultural backgrounds, experiences, and ideas. Diverse teams bring unique views that can help overcome biases and preconceptions.

8. **MAKE IDEAS VISIBLE**
   Share your ideas in simple, visual ways to ensure everyone understands. Sketching, video clips, or acting out ideas can be more effective than just talking about them.
9. **ACT AND LEARN**
   Try new approaches and learn from what happens. Running simple experiments shows what works and what doesn't.

These mindsets support a productive and innovative design thinking process, helping teams tackle challenges creatively and effectively.

You Can Do This Too

Learn design thinking and discover how to collaborate with people in your neighborhood to solve community problems. You and your team will design and build solutions that create a better and more equitable world.

You don't need extensive experience building things or inventing processes. Many of the student innovators in this book started with no experience but with a desire to make a difference. They began with hard work, creativity, and inspiration, along with duct tape, hot glue, and plenty of sticky notes. They brainstormed, tinkered, prototyped, experimented, and failed repeatedly until their solutions worked. They made a real difference in people's lives. If they can do it, you can do it.

Try an experiment. Close your eyes and imagine you and some friends working together to create a new device to help individuals. Maybe you create a new service that moves untouched leftover food from restaurants to food banks and shelters to feed people in your community. (One of my former students actually did this!)

In our world, progress, social justice, quality of life, and equity move forward one step at a time, one concerned team at a time, one good idea at a time, and one innovative project at a time. Your journey to make a difference starts now.

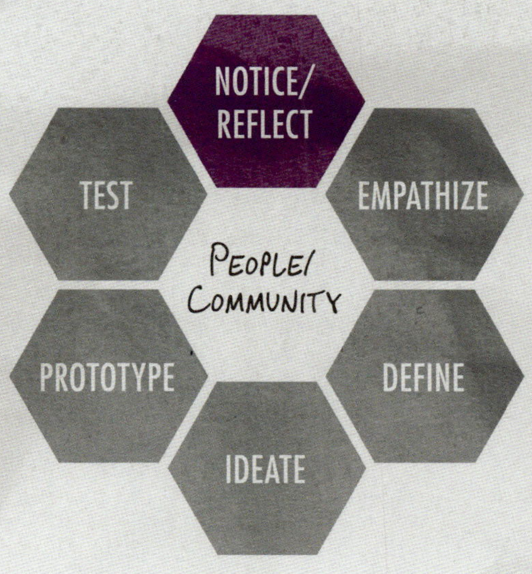

CHAPTER 1

Notice and Reflect

Knowing yourself is the beginning of all wisdom.

—ARISTOTLE

First seek to understand and then to be understood.

—STEPHEN COVEY

At the beginning of the design thinking process is the Notice and Reflect phase. The Notice and Reflect phase is foundational to equity-centered design. This phase guides designers to move beyond individual or small-group projects, challenging them first to look inward for self-awareness, then search outward for a broad, global consciousness of their intentions and actions.

Notice prompts designers to acknowledge their identity, values, assumptions, and biases. This self-awareness enables them to present their true selves, revealing both strengths and limitations. It creates a foundation that paves the way to approach design challenges with humility, curiosity, respect, and bravery.

This understanding prepares designers to address genuine needs rather than imposing their own preconceptions. For authentic empathy and collaboration, designers must recognize how their perspective aligns with or diverges from those of their community partners.

Reflect, the complementary component of this phase, involves continually assessing these principles throughout the design process. Designers and community partners collaboratively gauge the goals and outcomes of each phase, allowing for continual learning, ongoing improvements, and an unwavering commitment to equity, inclusivity, and global awareness.

Why Is Noticing and Reflecting So Important?

Adopting Notice and Reflect in the design process encourages design teams to consider ripple effects of their designs on the broader community. They may ask: What unintended consequences might occur? This process prompts designers to consider how their unique personal and cultural lenses shape their design choices. Moreover, it spurs them to factor in the global concerns of environmental impact and sustainability considerations, which are also firmly linked to equity.

One of the key benefits of community work is that it takes you outside of yourself and your comfort zone. It makes your world bigger as you help make the world better for others. With the community partners involved at every step, the final design is inclusive and equitable.

Preceding the Empathize phase, the Notice and Reflect phase is a bridge to a broader awareness of both the immediate community and overarching global issues. Return often, if only briefly, to revisit this phase throughout your design project. Your understanding of the underlying issues will grow as you design, and you may discover opportunities for systemic change. You may also see how to avoid unintended consequences.

You Are Here in the Design Thinking Process

This is the very beginning of the design thinking process. We start with noticing and reflecting on who we are, what we want to accomplish, and our position in a community and world we want to improve. From here, we move through the phases of design, though returning throughout to reconnect with our values.

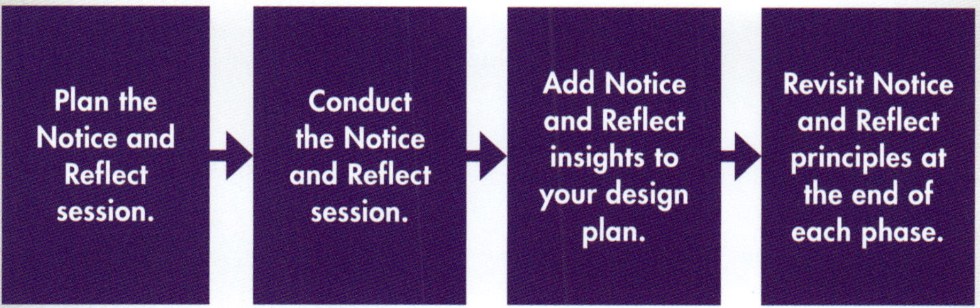

The activities in this chapter will enhance your own self-awareness and community consciousness, enabling you and your team to approach design challenges with a deeper understanding of and commitment to fairness, inclusivity, and societal impact. Specifically, you'll learn

- How your own identity, biases, and background influence your perspective and approach to design
- How to recognize social, political, and cultural factors that shape the challenges and opportunities of a community and your community partners
- How to ensure that the design process is rooted in fairness, inclusivity, and global consciousness
- Why it's crucial to continually reassess these considerations at each step in the design process

Time and Depth Guidelines

The amount of time to spend in the Notice and Reflect phase and the depth of your inquiry depend on your team as well as the nature and

Building Your Team

Starting an equity-centered design thinking project requires a strong, cohesive team. As you begin the Notice and Reflect phase, it's vital that your team members can trust one another, understand one another's strengths, and communicate effectively. Here's how you can get off to a strong start:

1. **Diversify your group.** Assemble a team that brings diverse perspectives in skills, experiences, or backgrounds. Diversity fosters creativity and ensures different viewpoints are considered.
2. **Set clear goals.** Before getting to work on tasks, have a team meeting to clarify what you aim to achieve. Aligning everyone's efforts toward a common goal helps ensure success.
3. **Define roles.** While flexibility is important, having clear roles can prevent overlap and ensure that every aspect of the project is covered. Roles can evolve, but having a starting point is crucial.
4. **Encourage open communication.** Create an environment where team members feel comfortable sharing ideas and giving feedback. This can be achieved through regular team meetings or casual check-ins.

scope of your design project. But every design project should engage with the Notice and Reflect phase sufficiently, since it sets the tone and direction for the entire design process. Here are some things to consider:

Nature of the Project

- Technical or specific solutions. Projects that are primarily technical and address a specific, defined problem—such as a fire sensor wristband for people who may not hear an alarm—might require less time in the Notice and Reflect phase. But even in these cases, time should be

5. **Establish conflict resolution.** Disagreements are bound to arise in any team setting. Establish a process to handle conflicts, ensuring that every voice is heard, and the focus remains on the project's objectives.
6. **Practice skill-building activities.** Lead the team in exercises or workshops that help team members build necessary skills, such as observational techniques or non-defensive listening for the Notice and Reflect phase or other technical skills for later phases.
7. **Bond with your team.** Integrate some fun activities or team-building exercises to foster trust, understanding, and camaraderie.
8. **Pause for reflection and feedback.** After major milestones, take a moment to reflect on what went well and what could be improved. This iterative feedback ensures continual improvement and adaptation.

The Notice and Reflect phase will bring out a lot of insights, emotions, and ideas. A cohesive team will be better equipped to handle the complexities and nuances this phase might unearth.

For more in-depth strategies and activities for team building, refer to IDEO's *Field Guide to Human-Centered Design* listed in the Going Further section.

dedicated to understanding the broader implications and potential unforeseen consequences. This is especially true if the design solution might be shared widely or become a commercial product.

- Community or systemic solutions. Projects such as the redesign of a neighborhood park or an after-school educational program affect larger groups and have systemic implications. These projects require a deeper understanding of community dynamics, history, culture, and multiple stakeholder perspectives, in addition to your community partners.

Familiarity with the Context

- High familiarity. If the design team is already familiar with the context or has prior experience with similar projects, they might need less time. However, it's important to validate prior knowledge. Things change.
- Low familiarity. If the context is new or unfamiliar, more time is needed to genuinely understand and empathize with systemic issues in the community.

Potential Impact and Scale

- Small-scale, direct impact. Projects with a direct and immediate impact on one individual or a small group might require less intensive reflection. For example, Team Stria wanted to design a device that would help their community partner, Javier, avoid veering into danger as he walked.
- Large-scale, broad impact. Projects that have the potential to affect large groups or have lasting impacts on communities or systems require more intensive reflection and engagement. What if the smart belt device for Javier could help many blind people avoid dangerous veering?

Stakeholder Involvement

- Directly involved community partners. If primary community partners such as Javier are directly involved in the design process, some elements of the Notice and Reflect phase, such as the research on the history of the issue in the region, might be streamlined.
- Multiple stakeholders. Projects with multiple stakeholders, such as for a redesign of a neighborhood park, will require more time in this phase to ensure all perspectives are considered. Also, intervention projects intended to stretch over longer periods require deeper inquiry.

Team Composition

- Diverse teams. Teams that are already diverse in terms of background, expertise, and perspective might navigate this phase faster.
- Homogeneous teams. Teams that lack diversity might need to invest more time to be sure they are culturally aware and consider a broad range of perspectives.

Troubleshooting during Notice and Reflect

Impatience to Move Forward

CHALLENGE

Teams may be eager to tackle the design and problem-solving stages right away, feeling that the Notice and Reflect phase is too introspective and slows down the process.

SOLUTION

First think about the scope of your project, using the guidelines above as a perspective. Then emphasize the long-term benefits of a solid foundation for your project. Rushing through or bypassing this phase may lead to challenges in working with your community partners or designs that lack cultural awareness or relevance to your community partners. Taking time to assess these needs at the start of the project saves time in later phases.

Navigating Sensitive Topics

CHALLENGE

Discussions may lead to sensitive or controversial topics, and teams might struggle with how to navigate these discussions, both within the design team and with community partners. Recognizing and admitting biases or preconceptions can be uncomfortable. Some people might become defensive or deny having any biases.

SOLUTION

Set ground rules for respectful discussions and create a safe, nonjudgmental environment. Emphasize that everyone has biases and that recognizing these biases is a strength, not a weakness. Consider consulting a facilitator or counselor who specializes in these discussions to help guide this process. Groups such as the National Equity Project provide training, resources, and workshops on effective noticing and reflection techniques.

Information Overwhelm

CHALLENGE

The process of noticing and reflecting can uncover a lot of information and sometimes lead to feeling overwhelmed or paralyzed.

SOLUTION

With the time and depth guidelines in mind, help the team to prioritize and categorize their findings. Break down the process into manageable, relevant steps, and ensure clear action points at each stage.

Steps in Notice and Reflect Phase

The Notice and Reflect phase lays the foundation for equity-centered design. During this phase, we think first about our personal perspectives and purposes before trying to understand the communities we're working with. Then our designs will truly align with the hopes and values of our community partners.

Notice

1. **CONSIDER HISTORY AND CONTEXT**

   Begin by understanding the history and context of your design challenge. Has it been shaped or influenced by societal, political, or cultural factors? A team discussion on what you already know can shed light on this. Quick

online research or a conversation with a community partner can fill in the blanks.

2. **IDENTIFY STAKEHOLDERS**

   Beyond your immediate community partners, who might benefit or be adversely affected by your solution? Pay attention to who is included in and who is excluded from the design process. Are you adequately considering the contributions and needs of those with less privilege? Drafting a list or mind map can help to visualize the broader ecosystem.

3. **ACKNOWLEDGE ASSUMPTIONS**

   Pause and pinpoint your preconceived notions about the community and stakeholders. For example, people who speak slowly often report that others sometimes assume slow speech indicates lower intelligence. Surface and then challenge assumptions like these, and look for ways to reduce unintentional bias.

4. **REVIEW LANGUAGE AND IMAGERY**

   Words and visuals have power. Consider how the language and imagery in the project may affect different groups. Consider the word *dumb*, which originally meant "unable to talk." But it quickly became entangled with the idea of *stupid*, or lacking intelligence—an implication it still carries.

   Ensure that the language and imagery associated with your project are respectful, inclusive, and empowering. Respectful language is not about "political correctness." It promotes kindness and consideration, and it projects positive intent.

5. **BECOME MORE SELF-AWARE**

   As mentioned, consider why you want to do this project and what you bring to it—both your assets and your limitations. Understand your identity, values, and assumptions. Recognizing and acknowledging these will pave the way for more genuine, equitable interactions with community partners.

Reflect

1. **APPLY YOUR OBSERVATIONS**
   Consider how to use your discoveries from the Notice stage to guide your design. How can we design to promote fairness and include everyone? How can we make our design work for all our community partners, regardless of background or identity?
2. **ASSESS COMMUNITY IMPACT**
   Anticipate how your design could affect various people in the larger community. Weigh the potential good and bad consequences of your design from a viewpoint of diversity and inclusion, as well as environmental impact and sustainability. Minimize any negative effects and increase the positive effects on different groups in the wider community. Ensure that any necessary trade-offs do not automatically favor more privileged groups.
3. **TRACK COMMUNITY FEEDBACK**
   As your design solution evolves during the Ideate and Prototype phases, talk to a variety of community members to get their thoughts and opinions on your design. Be open to feedback and constructive criticism. Look for ways to incorporate different viewpoints into your design process.
4. **EVALUATE CONTINUALLY**
   Regularly check on your design project at the close of each phase to ensure it's still promoting fairness and inclusion as well as stewardship of the environment. Gather data on how your design may affect different groups of people. Use this data to guide future versions of your design.

Design Project Journal

A design project journal can be an important tool in tracking your progress throughout your project and helping solve problems along the way. This journal documents lessons you've learned, how you solved certain problems, and why you made key design choices. It's a simple tool but an incredibly powerful way to capture your team's thoughts, insights, and reasoning.

Your design project journal can be a notebook or ring binder with handwritten or typed notes or a shared digital document, such as a Google Docs file. Either of these options work, so choose the one that best fits your team's needs.

Keep this documentation brief, taking fifteen to twenty minutes at the end of each phase. Your team can take turns with the recording. This is also a good point to refer to your community partner's Point of View (POV) Statement (see the Define chapter), as well as noticing and reflecting on your team process. It's OK that some phases may take longer to document than others.

Here are some general prompts to get you started:

- What surprised us in this phase?
- Which decisions were tough, and why did we choose the path we did?
- Were there any disagreements, and how did we resolve them?

As well as problems and issues, your journal can celebrate insights and innovative ideas. It's fun to go back and appreciate everyone's contributions and team victories.

Periodically revisit these journal entries, especially before significant decision points or when feeling stuck. It can provide fresh perspectives and jog memories. Over time, this journal becomes a stockpile of insights, patterns, and lessons learned that can be invaluable for training new team members or sharing the design thinking process with community partners or possible sponsors.

Non-Defensive Listening

Non-defensive listening is an invaluable skill in the Notice and Reflect phase of equity-centered design thinking, where the aim is to understand diverse perspectives and challenge personal biases. It facilitates open conversations, reduces misunderstandings, and fosters mutual respect. Here are some suggestions to help you improve your own skill:

- **Keep an open mind.** Approach conversations ready to hear viewpoints different from your own without immediate judgment.
- **Avoid interruptions.** Let speakers finish their point. Many people perceive interrupting as dismissive and disrespectful.
- **Use reflective feedback.** Rather than countering what someone says, try reflecting it back to ensure you've understood. For instance, "So, what I'm hearing is . . ."
- **Manage your emotional responses.** What someone says may trigger strong feelings, but it's essential to remain calm and composed. The focus should stay on understanding, not reacting. The classic technique of pausing and silently counting to ten before saying anything can help here.
- **Ask clarifying questions.** If something is unclear, ask open-ended questions. This shows you're engaged and interested in understanding better.
- **Avoid assumptions.** Don't fill in the gaps in the conversation, incomplete information, or unclear statements with your own assumptions and interpretations. If unsure, ask so you are sure you are getting the intended message.
- **Acknowledge the speaker.** Simple responses such as "Thank you for sharing that perspective" validate the speaker's experience and increase the connection.

Practicing non-defensive listening can be challenging, especially in conversations that touch on personal values or experiences. But mastering this skill is crucial for genuine collaboration and understanding in equity-centered design thinking.

5. **LOOK FOR BROADER IMPLICATIONS**
   Think about the larger social and cultural effects of your design project. Recognize how it relates to the broader themes of social justice, fairness, and environmental impact. Look for ways to use your design to help achieve larger social justice goals. Consider how your project might tie into other efforts to bring about social change.

By following these steps, designers and design teams can create more thoughtful and inclusive designs that consider the needs of all the stakeholders. This doesn't need to take a long time, but it will add depth and impact.

Before You Move On

Design thinking projects begin with the Notice and Reflect phase, the cornerstone of equity-centered design. We explore how Notice, the first part of this phase, prompts us as designers to look inward, acknowledging our own identities, biases, values, and assumptions. Reflect, the second part of this phase, encourages a habit of continual assessment, ensuring that principles of equity and inclusivity are woven into the fabric of the design process. Designers, in partnership with community stakeholders, collaboratively reflect on the goals and outcomes, fostering continual learning and a commitment to creating designs that are globally aware and just.

The importance of this phase of design thinking cannot be overstated. It encourages designers to consider the far-reaching impact of their designs, ensuring that solutions are inclusive, equitable, and mindful of their ripple effects. By stepping outside our comfort zones and embracing a broader perspective, we open ourselves up to creating designs that not only serve immediate needs but also contribute to a larger societal good.

Case Study: The Middle School Student Community Project

In 2013 middle school students in Oakland, California, wanted to design several small projects to improve the neighborhood around their school. But they knew they needed to learn more to make their project a success, so they used the principles of the Notice and Reflect phase to tackle essential questions before beginning their fieldwork. They considered these questions:

- What constitutes a community?
- Who plays a role in a community, and what are their stakes?
- What are the fundamental needs every community has?

These discussions built on talks earlier in the year about preconceptions, biases, and assumptions, as well as previous grounding in cultural awareness.

Armed with a better understanding and guided by these questions, the students researched more about the complex history of this area, using both online searches and library media resources.

Next, they divided the neighborhood into four sections, with a student team each focusing on a section. They gathered information about the neighborhood from direct observation and interviews with residents and business owners.

As they explored their designated areas, they carefully documented their findings with photos, sketches, and detailed notes. They even joined the local online community forum to hear more voices from the neighborhood.

These students discovered that individuals in a community have distinct viewpoints and experiences based on their specific roles, such as resident, business owner, customer, visitor, student, or worker. Their comprehensive approach provided invaluable firsthand insights about their neighborhood and prepared them for a successful design project.

Students gather to share and reflect on their thoughts after surveying a local community park.

After gathering and examining their research data, four middle school student community action teams identified needs in their part of the neighborhood. The teams then created 3D models of projects that could improve the area. These models included a dog park, community garden, small police station, and crosswalk at a local intersection.

The students showcased their project models at a meeting with school and community members. Their presentation prompted appreciation from the group and sparked lively discussion. This process allowed students to receive opinions and feedback about their designs, and learn about how to identify community problems and design solutions.

The goal of the Notice and Reflect phase ensures our design work and the final design are fair, considerate, and in line with our values, as the Oakland middle school students demonstrated.

The Notice and Reflect phase flows into the Empathize phase, where we'll put our heightened self-awareness and global consciousness into practice, aiming for solutions that resonate on a deeper, more meaningful level with our community partners. Come back to the Notice and Reflect phase as a touchpoint throughout the design process to remain aligned with our values and the wider community's needs.

Notice and Reflect Checklist

- ⬡ Have you taken the time to understand your own biases, values, and cultural perspectives?
- ⬡ Have you considered how these factors might influence your design decisions?
- ⬡ Have you met with your design team to determine the best time and depth for your Notice and Reflect phase activities?
- ⬡ Did the team collaboratively engage in the Notice and Reflect phase appropriate for your project's context?
- ⬡ Have you considered how insights from the Notice and Reflect phase will shape and inform your design approach?
- ⬡ Have you identified the potential impact of your project on the broader community, in addition to your immediate community partners?
- ⬡ Are there plans in place to revisit the Notice and Reflect phase considerations at the conclusion of each project phase?

Reflection Questions

- How has the Notice and Reflect phase challenged or expanded your understanding of design thinking?
- Why is it important to continually return to the Notice and Reflect phase throughout the design process?
- How do personal identity and background influence design decisions? Can you provide an example from your own experience or observations?
- How does the concept of global consciousness fit into the Notice and Reflect phase, and why is it crucial for equity-centered design?
- How do you think the dynamics of a design team might change after undergoing the Notice and Reflect phase?

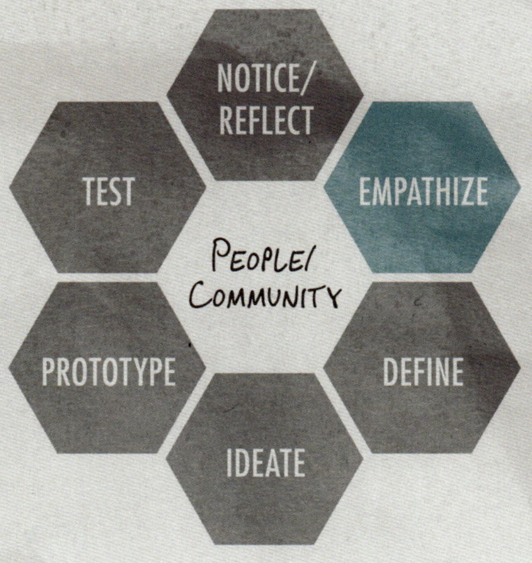

CHAPTER 2

Empathize

Empathy is about finding echoes of another person in yourself.

—MOHSIN HAMID

You can observe a lot by just watching.

—YOGI BERRA, A FAMOUS BASEBALL PLAYER

To empathize is to see the world through someone else's eyes, sense their emotions, and connect with their experiences. While people often use the terms *sympathy*, *empathy*, and *compassion* interchangeably, they are different. Sympathy means to feel sorry for someone else's situation. Empathy entails understanding and sharing the feelings of another. Compassion is an awareness of another's distress with a desire to alleviate it.

The Empathize phase in design thinking involves immersing ourselves in the lives of community partners to grasp their challenges, desires, and aspirations. Beyond understanding on a surface level, empathy is a more profound, personal comprehension.

Why Is Empathy So Important?

Imagine visiting a doctor who hastily scribbles a prescription without asking any questions or examining you. You would likely feel unheard and skeptical of their expertise and advice. Similarly, community partners want solutions for their specific situation. We all want to work with people who know *us* as individuals.

Our goal is not just to make or change something—it is to design an innovation that improves people's lives. Empathizing creates a detailed picture of the needs of the community partner and grounds the entire project in the community partner's world, distinguishing design thinking from other problem-solving.

You Are Here in the Design Thinking Process

As you begin the Empathize phase, you've already identified your community partners and have a foundational understanding of the challenge ahead. You move beyond mere understanding to genuine empathy, deepening your connection with your community partners and their needs.

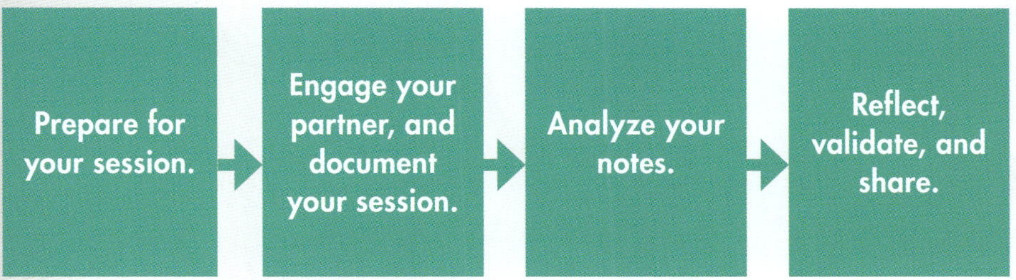

These techniques will help you learn more about your community partners and the context of the problems faced, specifically these:

- How to gather data using interviews, focus groups, observations, and immersion activities
- How to analyze this data to gain a deeper understanding of your community partners and their situation

Mind Maps

A mind map is a practical tool used to organize information visually around a central concept or problem, which is written inside a circle or box at the center of a blank page. Related ideas or subtopics stem out from this central concept, connected by lines or branches that signify their relationship to the main idea and one another.

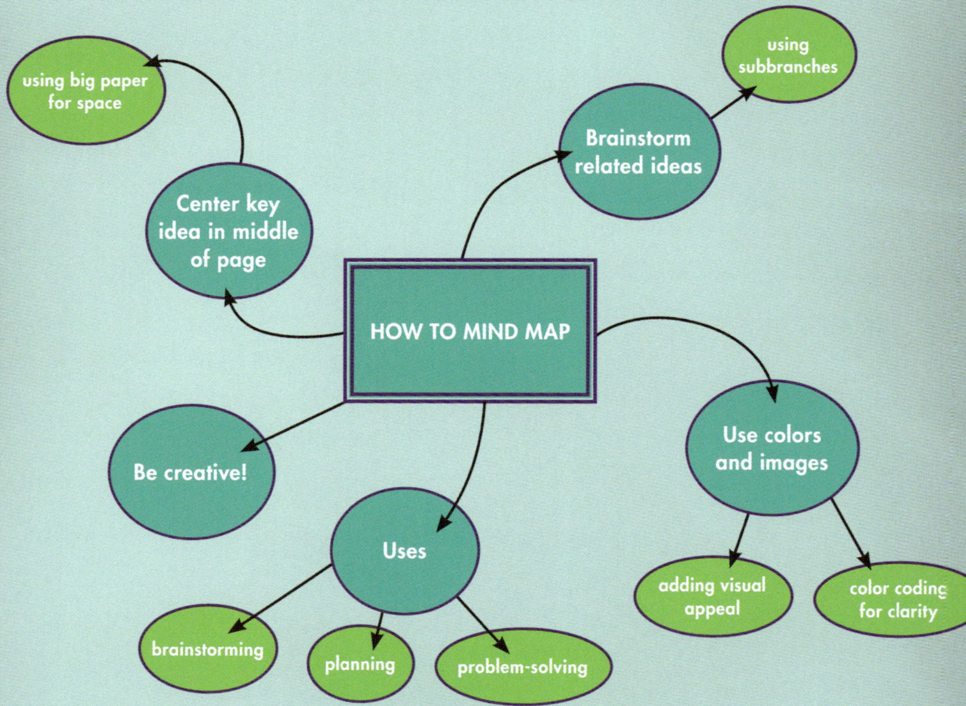

Each of these subtopics can also branch out into related ideas, creating weblike structures that mirror the nonlinear way our brains work. Mind maps often radiate outward from the central box like spokes on a bicycle wheel, although some may take on a tree or organization-chart structure.

A mind map's key strength lies in fostering creative thinking by enabling designers to see the connections and relationships among different ideas.

For example, if a design thinker is exploring concepts for a new eco-friendly product, they might start with "sustainable materials" in the central box. Branching out from this main idea, they could list different types of sustainable materials, and further subbranches may include specific products made from each material. Through this process, relationships and patterns emerge to spark new avenues of thought.

The effectiveness of a mind map often increases with its visual richness. Adding color, symbols, and images engages the brain in a creative, intuitive way to enhance both idea generation and memory recall.

Here are some steps to create a mind map:

1. **Start with a central idea or topic.** This is the focus of your mind map. Write it in a circle or a box in the center of your page.
2. **Brainstorm related ideas.** Think of all the different aspects of your central idea. Write these ideas as branches coming out of the central circle or box.
3. **Expand on your ideas.** For each branch, brainstorm even more specific ideas. You can use subbranches to organize your ideas.
4. **Use images and colors.** Mind maps are more visually appealing and easier to remember when you use images, symbols, and colors.
5. **Be creative.** There is no right or wrong way to make a mind map. Be creative and have fun with it!

Here are some additional tips for making a mind map:

- Use a large piece of paper so you have plenty of space.
- Use different colors to represent different ideas or concepts.
- Use images to make your mind map more visually appealing.
- Don't be afraid to add new ideas or branches as you think of them.

The versatile nature of mind maps makes them an invaluable tool throughout the design thinking process, from initial brainstorming sessions through complex problem-solving to the final stages of project planning.

- How to create mind maps, empathy maps, and journey maps and use them during empathy research and then throughout the design process

This emphasis on better understanding of your community partners distinguishes design thinking from other problem-solving processes. These understandings set the stage for transformative solutions that extend well beyond the immediate problem and contribute to broader social change.

Troubleshooting Empathy Challenges

The Empathize phase in design thinking can present certain unique challenges, given its emphasis on genuine human understanding and connection. Here are some potential challenges and tips for handling them:

Difficulty Accessing Needed Participants

CHALLENGE

Your empathy research depends on working with informed participants, which may make it more difficult to find appropriate people.

SOLUTION

First keep trying and be flexible about dates, since everyone is busy. Be sure they know the "why" of your research, so they are more likely to care about "what" you want to know. If they are not available, move down your list to the next best sources. Alternatively, use secondary research or expert interviews, while always acknowledging the limitations. Try more digital immersion—covered below—and immersive visits to the community. As often happens on such visits, you may meet just the right person.

Bias and Assumption

CHALLENGE

Design thinkers may unintentionally allow personal biases or preexisting assumptions to color their understanding.

SOLUTION

Maintain an open-minded "beginner's mindset." Engage in reflective practices from the Notice and Reflect chapter, and encourage peer reviews to uncover unintentional biases.

Overwhelming Amounts of Data

CHALLENGE

Overly broad data collected during empathy research may lead to analysis paralysis.

SOLUTION

Use categorization, prioritize based on relevance, and employ visualization tools such as mind maps to distill and simplify data.

People Problems in Empathy Research

CHALLENGE

Sometimes gathering information from participants is difficult.

SOLUTION

If the interview or focus group is not getting at genuine feelings or motivations, try using open-ended questions. You can also encourage storytelling and create a safe and comfortable environment for participants.

Some participants require more space and processing time to give the most helpful responses. They may prefer to get questions in advance, a quiet environment, and more time between questions. You can also encourage such participants by giving them a low pressure environment to generate thoughtful responses. Sometimes, allowing people to respond in writing may yield better results.

Some highly expressive people may inadvertently dominate the conversation in a focus group. Calmly but firmly remind them of the ground rules about participation and the value of hearing all voices.

Emotional Burnout

CHALLENGE

Empathy can sometimes lead to emotional fatigue for you and your team, especially when dealing with challenging experiences with your community partners.

SOLUTION

Encourage regular reflection and debriefing sessions for the team. Provide a supportive environment where team members can express and process their feelings about the project. Take breaks for rest and fun.

Differing Interpretations from Team Members

CHALLENGE

Different team members might come away from the same interaction with widely varying interpretations as to what is going on and how to best proceed.

SOLUTION

Regular team huddles to discuss findings and sync interpretations help ensure a more unified collective understanding. Review the specific data together with an open mind. Embrace diverse perspectives, as they can lead to richer insights.

Steps in Empathize Phase

The Empathize phase requires thinking ahead and engaging fully with others. This structured approach guides you through the process.

1. **PREPARE FOR THE EMPATHY SESSION**

   Before beginning an actual empathy session, know what you're aiming to achieve. Start by defining the specific objectives you want to accomplish during this phase. What do you need to learn from your community partner? Which aspects of their experience are essential for your project?

   Once you've clarified these goals, plan out your session. Decide whether to use interviews, focus groups, observations, immersion activities, or some combination of these. The Gathering Empathy Data sections beginning on page 46 describe each technique, when to use it, and how to use it.

   Also, set a date, time, and location that's convenient for your community partner. Now you are ready.

2. **ENGAGE YOUR PARTNER AND DOCUMENT YOUR SESSION**

   Engaging genuinely and actively with your community partner is the heart of the Empathize phase. Start your session by building rapport. Your goal is to make your community partner feel comfortable and valued. In an interview or focus group, listen more than you speak and let them lead the conversation. Encourage them to tell stories, which convey more than a simple description of the facts.

   As you meet, document the session carefully. Take notes, record voice memos, or capture photos or videos—always asking permission first.

3. **ANALYZE YOUR NOTES**

   After the session, sort through the information you've gathered. Lay out all your notes, recordings, photos, and any other data you've collected. Look for patterns, problems, and insights that can guide your design project. Group similar ideas and create visual representations such as mind maps or empathy maps.

Case Study: The Breathing Tube

Deyon needs to stay alert to take care of the critical needs of his son, Jomari, who has cerebral palsy. Jomari is quadriplegic and cannot move on his own. To breathe, Jomari has a tracheotomy tube in his throat. But mucus continually accumulates in his throat and breathing tube, blocking his airway. Deyon needs to clear Jomari's throat tube every few hours, day and night. Deyon gets just three and a half hours of sleep every night, which is frequently interrupted. This affects his health and leaves him perpetually groggy.

"How many hours of sleep did you get last night? I got four, and I'm barely awake," Sam remarked, having purposefully limited the number of hours he slept to better understand the effects of sleep deprivation. Sam, along with Preston, Eliot, and Kate from Team Syphon, wanted to help Deyon care for his son and himself. How could they help make life better for this family?

The members of Team Syphon got to know Deyon's and Jomari's daily lives and really understood the challenges they faced, especially the requirements of Jomari's health condition. Their empathy research and time spent with the family enabled the team to design a sensor-activated suctioning device. It allows Jomari to feel more secure and Deyon to sleep knowing Jomari is safe.

Team Syphon displays their device at Demo Day.

4. **REFLECT, VALIDATE, AND SHARE**

   After your analysis, take a step back and reflect. Does everything make sense? Do you see any gaps or areas that might need further exploration? Check back with your community partners to verify your analysis and conclusions. Revisit any unclear points from your discussions or observations.

   Once you and your team are confident in your findings, share them with your community partners and stakeholders. As a group, reach a consensus, finding a common ground that respects the views and opinions of all participants. This often involves discussion, negotiation, and sometimes compromise to arrive at a decision that satisfies all parties involved. Then move forward, confident that everyone can accept and support the plan.

The Empathize phase is dynamic. You might find that after reflecting, you need to return to earlier steps, adjust your approach, or ask new questions. Flexibility and a genuine desire to understand your community partners are crucial in making this phase effective and productive.

Empathy Research Tools

This chapter will cover two parts of empathy research: gathering empathy data and analyzing it. Several of these tools and techniques will appear first in this chapter and relate to later design thinking process phases, such as the Define or Ideate phases.

There is no fixed order to using these data-gathering tools, and you can pick a place to start based on your sense of the situation. You will probably use more than one tool for your project, and it is often useful to combine tools. For example, you may have several interviews, perhaps with patients at a community clinic, then visit that clinic to observe the patient experience.

You may also use the same tool more than once. For example, you may do some interviews and, using what you learn, conduct a focus group. During the focus group, you may see that one participant has superb insights and then follow up afterward with an interview with that person.

During the analysis step of the Empathize phase, the designers organize the experiences, emotions, perceptions, and ideas of community partners and other stakeholders about the problem into a coherent picture, guiding the next steps.

We will start by summarizing these four main data-gathering tools and when and how to use them before explaining how to analyze your findings:

- Interviews
- Focus groups
- Observations
- Immersion activities

Gathering Empathy Data: INTERVIEWS

An empathy interview offers valuable insight at various stages of data collection by investigating unanswered questions or probing complex issues more deeply. Designers listen actively, encourage storytelling, and often use open-ended questions to gain deep understanding of experiences, feelings, needs, and perspectives. These might not surface in more structured interviews.

The interviewer must be sure to prioritize asking the most important questions and not digress too much. This open-ended form of interview emphasizes the "why" behind behaviors and choices.

Interviews typically last thirty to sixty minutes, depending on the interviewee and what you hope to learn. Sometimes, multiple sessions might be necessary. Make sure the person is open to answering follow-up questions. Conducting multiple interviews might reveal patterns over time and allow for question adjustments.

For example, Team Syphon interviewed Deyon to learn about his life and experience as a caregiver for Jomari, along with learning more about keeping Jomari's airway clear. Team Alertra, whom you'll meet in the Ideate chapter, interviewed firefighters to learn more about the hazards and issues people who are hard of hearing face during home fires.

Most empathy research uses interviews at some point since they work very well for in-depth conversations with individual community partners. They also adapt easily to your research goals. You might have interviews with several community partners to get different perspectives. You might also request a follow-up interview to go deeper into a topic that came up in a first interview.

A successful empathy interview builds trust, avoids judgment, and approaches the conversation with genuine curiosity.

Planning the Interview

1. **ESTABLISH CLEAR OBJECTIVES**

   Before you start, be clear about what you want to learn. What are you trying to understand about their experience and perspective?

2. **CRAFT OPEN-ENDED QUESTIONS**

   Prepare questions that require more than a simple yes or no. For instance, don't ask "Is this a problem for the neighborhood?" That question may get just a yes or no answer. Try phrasing the question as "How do you feel about this situation in the neighborhood?" Ask for in-depth examples. Test your questions with a friend to find weak or obvious questions.

3. **ALLOW FOR FLEXIBILITY**

   While you'll prepare some questions in advance, be ready to adapt based on where the conversation goes. This is the essence of a responsive interview.

4. **SELECT A COMFORTABLE ENVIRONMENT**

Choose a location where your community partner feels at ease and can speak freely. This might be at their home, a community center, or even a local café.

Remote interviews via platforms such as Zoom, although less personal, allow you to interview people who are not available for an in-person meeting. Regardless of the medium, minimize potential disruptions.

5. **GATHER NECESSARY MATERIALS**

Consider how you'll document the conversation: note-taking, video, or audio recording? Video and audio recordings are less disruptive, so you can engage more fully in the conversation. If you wish to record the conversation—which can be very useful—get the interviewee's permission beforehand.

Assure them that you will only use the recording during the design project, and it won't appear anywhere else, such as on social media. Will you destroy the recording after you complete the project? This helps people feel more comfortable and speak more candidly.

For some interviews, you may need to take notes. It is important to write legibly and review notes immediately after the interview. You can also have one team member conduct the interview, while another takes notes.

If you have recorded the interview, you may want a transcript afterward. Transcription is time-consuming but can help you glean valuable bits of information. Transcription services offer high accuracy and quick turnaround but may cost more than your budget allows. Another alternative is voice-to-text software, which can be free or low cost. As with any transcription, read the transcript carefully and verify it for accuracy.

Conducting the Interview

1. **BUILD RAPPORT**

   Begin by ensuring your community partner feels safe and comfortable in the interview setting. Remind them they can pass on a question or end the interview at any time.

   Start with simple, factual questions before diving into more complex or personal ones. Be friendly and genuinely curious, as well as respectful and nonjudgmental. The participant should feel comfortable sharing their thoughts and feelings, even if they are negative. Approach the interview as if you're having an engaging conversation with a friend about an important topic.

2. **LISTEN ACTIVELY**

   Listen more than you speak. Use body language such as nodding and maintaining eye contact to show you're listening closely. If your interviewee feels as if you don't care about what they are saying, they will not fully engage.

   Let your community partner guide the direction, and make sure to return to important unanswered questions.

3. **USE FOLLOW-UP QUESTIONS**

   As the interview progresses, be ready to follow intriguing leads that depart from your planned questions—the beauty of a responsive interview lies in its adaptability. If your interviewee brings up a topic you hadn't considered as the conversation progresses, explore it.

   Take advantage of opportunities to ask follow-up questions. If something is interesting or unclear, ask them to elaborate or clarify. For instance, follow up on responses with questions such as, "Can you tell me more about that?" or "Why do you feel that way?" Be prepared to follow a new line of questioning.

4. **ALLOW FOR SILENCES**
   Sometimes, people need a moment to think before they answer. Don't rush to fill every pause.
5. **AVOID ASSUMPTIONS**
   If your partner mentions something you're not familiar with, ask them to explain rather than making assumptions. These assumptions may allow biases to creep in.
6. **WRAP UP GRACEFULLY**
   As the interview concludes, thank them for their time and insights. Summarize the next steps and how you will use their input.
7. **REFLECT AFTER THE SESSION**
   Once the interview is over, spend time considering the responses. What did you learn? Were there any surprises? What new questions emerged? Are you getting the answers you need? If not, refine your questions and ask the person for a follow-up interview or interview someone else who might know. Be sure to thank everyone you interview.

Gathering Empathy Data: FOCUS GROUPS

A design thinking focus group gathers a small group of community partners to discuss their experiences, share stories, and provide insight about the problem.

A facilitator guides the discussion using open-ended questions and keeps conversation moving in a productive direction. Ideally, the conversation develops naturally as the participants respond. The facilitator engages with participants' input without dominating the discussion. The facilitator also encourages quieter members to contribute their insights and persuades more vocal members to share the conversation.

Focus groups have several advantages. Engaging multiple community partners simultaneously can lead to a rich, interactive

discussion, and one person's comment might spark insights from another person. You can gather information from several participants in a relatively short time.

Additionally, observing interactions and discussions among participants can reveal group attitudes, shared values, and collective challenges. The way someone talks about a topic, their body language, and their interactions can provide context beyond their words alone.

When to Use a Focus Group

Focus groups can complement interviews. For example, focus groups would work well for the Oakland middle school students learning about the wants and needs of the community in the neighborhood park redesign. We know they interviewed residents, business owners, visitors, and workers to get different perspectives, but we don't know if they used focus groups.

A focus group can put people with various social roles in the same conversation so everyone can hear different perspectives and work together toward mutually agreeable solutions. If you only use interviews of individuals in research, you will miss responses and ideas created when people interact with one another.

Conducting a Focus Group

Much like organizing a good interview, conducting a successful focus group requires careful planning and skillful facilitation to achieve meaningful results. Here's a structured approach adapted for the dynamics of a small group:

1. **SET YOUR OBJECTIVES**

   Start by clearly stating what you want to learn. Draft open-ended questions to guide the discussion. You need fewer questions than in one-on-one interviews since several people may respond to any question. Use a mind map (see page 38) to organize your thoughts. Test your questions informally with friends to test their responses and understand how the group may interact.

2. **RECRUIT AND SELECT PARTICIPANTS**

   Aim for a diverse group of five to ten people to provide varied experiences and perspectives on the topic. Avoid large power imbalances among the participants. Interviewing authority figures separately can prevent them from having undue influence on how others respond.

   The ideal focus group duration is between sixty to ninety minutes. This allows enough time for everyone to express their views but does not drag out the discussion.

3. **DEVELOP A DISCUSSION GUIDE**

   Frame questions as open-ended to prompt in-depth discussions and storytelling. Organize questions from broad to specific, letting participants ease into deeper discussions. Visual aids or props can prompt discussion.

4. **SET THE ENVIRONMENT**

   Choose a quiet, comfortable location where participants will feel at ease sharing their thoughts and talking openly. Arrange seating so everyone can see one another to encourage dialogue. Consider providing refreshments for a relaxed atmosphere.

   Virtual focus groups can work, especially if time is short or if people are not in the same place. But virtual focus groups are not as personal and often not as richly detailed. Choose whether the group is all in-person or all virtual, since mixing the two creates an uncomfortable group dynamic where the virtual participants feel their input is less valued.

5. **FACILITATE THE FOCUS GROUP**

   Begin with introductions and explain the focus group's purpose within the larger project. Set ground rules for respect and active listening. The facilitator remains neutral, guiding the conversation without imposing opinions. Use probing questions such as "Can you tell me more?" to delve deeper. Be flexible, deviating from the guide if the conversation reveals valuable insights.

   Encourage participants to put away distractions, such as cell phones. Ensure everyone can contribute with no one monopolizing the discussion. Change topics only when all have spoken or if talking points become repetitive. Prioritize understanding and insights and avoid seeking consensus. Brainstorming solutions comes later. Monitor the clock to respect everyone's schedule, and thank participants at the end.

6. **DOCUMENT YOUR SESSION**

   If everyone consents, record the focus group discussion to make analysis easier after the session. If you are not recording, ask someone on your design team to be a notetaker. They should note nonverbal cues and body language in addition to what people say. Afterward, jot down any immediate thoughts or impressions for later analysis.

7. **FOLLOW UP**

   Thank participants and let them know you will keep them informed about how the input will be used. This promotes goodwill and continued engagement. Conduct follow-up interviews with people who have specific thoughts or ideas worth investigating with more depth.

With careful planning and execution, a focus group provides deep, varied insights into your design issue. Conducting an effective focus group is a skill you continue to develop with practice. Use the insights gained from the focus group to inform the Define and Ideate phases of your design thinking process.

Gathering Empathy Data: OBSERVATIONS

In the design thinking process, observation means carefully watching and studying community partners in their natural environment. Instead of solely relying on what community partners say, observation focuses on understanding their actions, behaviors, habits, routines, and the context in which they normally operate. This method provides designers with a better understanding of real-world challenges, interactions, and potential problems.

For example, Chris and Danita wanted to help an older person live independently in his own home. After interviewing him and his adult daughter, who lived nearby, they observed him at home as he went about his daily routines. They watched him make food, use appliances, and clean up in the kitchen. Throughout the house, they noted potential hazards, such as loose rugs, hard corners, sharp objects, or hot surfaces.

Through their observations, Danita and Chris saw firsthand the struggles he experienced. Using their notes and some ingenuity, they made various modifications to make this man's home safer, more comfortable, and more livable for him.

When to Use Observations

Observations provide invaluable insights by offering a window into the lives of community partners and can help design solutions grounded in their needs and lives. Here are some benefits of observations:

1. **TO SEE WHAT'S HIDING IN PLAIN VIEW**
   Your community partners may struggle to recognize or express their needs. By observing, you can uncover these and see firsthand how they navigate their issues.

2. **TO UNDERSTAND THE FULL PICTURE**
   Observations help you grasp the context in which your community partners encounter their problems. Recognizing the physical, social, or cultural factors shaping their experience allows you to craft tailor-made solutions for their real-life environment.
3. **TO SPOT THE GAP**
   What people say they do and what they *actually* do can be very different. Observations help you spot these inconsistencies.
4. **TO UNEARTH HIDDEN GEMS**
   As you watch your community partners closely, you might stumble upon needs or opportunities for innovation that even they hadn't thought of.

How to Conduct an Observation

When conducting observations for design thinking, consider the following steps:

1. **DEFINE OBJECTIVES**
   Understand what you're hoping to learn. What specifically are you looking for? What do you expect to see, and what insights are you hoping to gain? Are you looking for problems in a process? Behavioral patterns? Interactions with specific objects or features in the setting?
2. **CHOOSE THE RIGHT ENVIRONMENT**
   Whenever possible, observe people in the setting where the activity or process you're interested in typically occurs.
3. **WATCH ATTENTIVELY AND (MAYBE) ASK QUESTIONS**
   There are two major ways to observe your community partners: the silent "fly on the wall" approach or the talk-aloud method.

In a silent observation, the observer does not interact with the individual being observed or the setting. A silent observation offers an authentic glimpse into your community partner's experience as they follow their natural behavioral patterns.

A talk-aloud method combines an interview and an observation to witness the challenges faced by your community partner firsthand. Note their actions, comments, facial expressions, and body language. Ask them to describe their thoughts and feelings as they follow their normal process. Pose open-ended questions to encourage detailed responses, and ask follow-up questions as needed.

For example, the daily job of operating and cleaning a complicated coffee maker may be difficult for a person with arthritis. You could ask the person to describe each step and highlight any obstacles they encounter. Verbalizing may make them more aware of each action and the potential barriers, shedding light on critical details that they might not bring up in other contexts due to their familiarity with the task.

4. **NOTE YOUR OBSERVATIONS**

Decide how you'll document the process. Will you record the observation on video or take notes and photos? Trying to take notes while observing can be difficult, and you risk missing important parts of the scenario. If your community partner gives explicit permission to record video, you can replay and review these videos later. Note nonverbal cues, interactions, and even what's not happening, which can be just as revealing.

5. **SUSPEND JUDGMENTS**

   Avoid making immediate judgments or interpretations during the observation. Your goal is to capture the actual behavior. After observing, jot down any immediate thoughts or impressions for later analysis.

6. **RESPECT PRIVACY**

   When conducting an observation, always keep ethical considerations in mind. Informed consent from those being observed is required. Aim to maintain a fair perspective and avoid bias. Consider your point of view in an observation. Allow people to opt out whenever they wish.

   Observation offers a unique lens into the daily realities and experiences of users. When combined with other empathy-building tools such as interviews and immersion, it provides a big-picture understanding that can inspire innovative solutions.

Gathering Empathy Data: IMMERSION ACTIVITIES

Immersion activities are direct, hands-on experiences that allow design thinkers to walk in the shoes of their community partners. Unlike observations, immersion involves actively taking part in the everyday lives of those people they seek to understand—whether it's spending a day performing a specific job, using a product or service in its intended environment, or engaging in the routines of a particular community.

This way, designers gain a more personal understanding of the challenges, needs, and motivations of community partners.

When to Use Immersion Activities

1. **TO DEEPEN UNDERSTANDING**

   Immersion offers a depth of insight that's hard to achieve with interviews or observations.

2. **TO HELP SOLVE COMPLEX CHALLENGES**
   For intricate problems where the context is as important as the challenge itself, immersion can reveal underlying factors and subtleties. When a community partner says, "It's difficult to explain unless you have been there," immersion might help.
3. **TO BRIDGE CULTURAL OR EXPERIENCE GAPS**
   In projects where community partners have a vastly different lifestyle, culture, or language than those in the design team, immersion helps break down assumptions and fosters genuine understanding. Always undertake these deep immersion experiences in close collaboration with community partners and with the highest level of respect.
4. **TO INSPIRE INNOVATIVE SOLUTIONS**
   When aiming for breakthrough solutions or new perspectives, immersing oneself can spark fresh ideas by experiencing some part of a community partner's world.

How to Conduct Immersion Activities

1. **SET CLEAR OBJECTIVES**
   Know what you hope to achieve. Is it to understand a specific challenge? To experience a daily routine? To see how a product integrates into daily life? Having a clear focus ensures you gain relevant insights. The choice of immersion method should align with the project's goals.
2. **BE RESPECTFUL AND ETHICAL**
   Remember, you're entering someone else's space and life. Always seek permission, be respectful of boundaries, and ensure your immersion doesn't disrupt or inconvenience them.

3. **DOCUMENT EVERYTHING**
   While it's crucial to be present and engaged, also document your experiences. This can be through notes, photos, or voice recordings with the permission of all participants. These will be invaluable when reflecting later.
4. **STAY OPEN AND CURIOUS**
   Immersion is as much about feeling as it is about observing. Stay open to new experiences, ask questions, and be genuinely curious. Resist the urge to jump to solutions, since this phase is about understanding.
5. **REFLECT AND DEBRIEF**
   After the immersion, reflect on what you've experienced. Discuss with your team, share insights, and identify patterns or surprises that emerged.

Consider a Range of Immersion Activities

In **shadowing**, a designer follows a community partner for a day. Studies that use neuroimaging techniques such as fMRI and EEG have consistently shown that imagining an activity leads to stronger and more widespread brain activation compared to just watching it. This suggests that the brain is more deeply engaged when we imagine ourselves doing something, recruiting additional areas involved in memory, emotion, and self-awareness.

In **participatory immersion**, the designer actively engages in the daily tasks or routines of a community partner. This involves literally doing the activity alongside the community partner. For instance, if a community partner is a farmer, the designer might spend a day working on the farm to understand the challenges of farming.

Situational immersion puts the designer in specific situations or scenarios that the community partner faces. For instance, to understand challenges people with mobility issues face, a designer might use a wheelchair for a day.

Cultural immersion involves taking part in the cultural and societal context of the community. For example, the group working on the community park in Oakland visited local events and festivals to understand more about the community the park would serve.

Role-playing is a more controlled form of immersion. Designers simulate a scenario in collaboration with community partners and play different roles to empathize with a new perspective.

With the aid of technology, **digital immersion** allows designers to immerse themselves in the digital platforms or environments of their community partners. The Oakland students visited community websites and read newsletters and local publications to increase their understanding of community challenges and needs.

Immersion is powerful but should be part of a broader empathy tool kit. Combine insights from immersion with those from interviews, observations, and other empathy exercises to get a holistic understanding.

Analysis: DISCOVERING THEMES AND GENERATING INSIGHTS

Empathy research doesn't end with data collection. You must make sense of that data and learn from it. Recognizing when to shift from collecting to analyzing data and making sense of it is an essential step in design thinking.

When interviews, observations, focus groups, and immersion activities yield repetitive or familiar information, it's a sign that you've covered enough ground with data collection and it's time to shift to analysis. Since design thinking is iterative, you can always integrate new findings later.

When analyzing empathy data, do the following:

1. **BE OPEN-MINDED**

   Don't let preconceived notions limit your interpretation of data. Be open to new ideas and insights.

2. **BE CREATIVE**
   Look for patterns and connections that aren't immediately obvious. What new insights can you generate?
3. **BE COLLABORATIVE**
   Seek feedback from your team members and community partners. Different perspectives often shed new light on the data.

Your goal is to gain a deeper understanding of your community partners and to create better, more empathetic solutions.

Tackling the Data Analysis

1. **THEMATIC IDENTIFICATION**
   Themes are recurring patterns that offer insights into the desires, needs, and challenges faced by your community partners.
   For instance, while aiding an elderly man who wanted to continue to live independently in his own home, Danita and Chris observed several difficulties posed by his daily routine. Over a lifetime, he acquired many kitchen tools and appliances. Arthritis has hindered his ability to use some, while others were difficult to locate in the clutter.
   Creating themes such as "clutter," "hard to operate," and "safety issues," the team started a plan for their community partner.
2. **VISUAL REPRESENTATION**
   Begin by laying out all your collected data visually. Spread out photographs, documents, sketches, and other visual aids.
   If you're collaborating with a team, ensure everyone has access to the interview transcripts, observation notes, and any statistical analysis that's been done.

Display physical items prominently for all to see. Think of setting up an "insight wall," much like a detective's evidence board. If your data is digital, platforms such as Jamboard or Mural can help.

3. **DELIBERATION AND DEBRIEFING**

   After collecting data, regroup and reflect. What stood out? Did anything surprise you or contradict your initial assumptions? Recognizing these insights early can shape your next steps and overall design strategy.

4. **ANALYSIS AND SYNTHESIS**

   Review all materials meticulously, looking for patterns, insights, and new themes while you categorize the data. Approach these themes with an open mind since new insights often emerge from unexpected places.

   Listen to the tone of recorded interviews and conversations, and take note of what's left unsaid—not just the words. Notice any personal bias or unjustified assumptions that may have clouded perception of the data and might slant the analysis.

   Review the data as a team to combine both individual reflection and group discussions, ensuring a variety of perspectives. You're not just looking for the most common answers but also for insights that can lead to innovative solutions.

   Check the data with your community partners, both to validate the accuracy and to generate new insights. This also inspires greater trust.

   Prioritize these insights according to the relevance of your partners' needs or potential impact on the design.

Returning to the example of our team helping the elderly man stay in his home, Danita and Chris realized the need to simplify

and organize his home and replace some of his possessions.

They helped him replace heavy cast-iron pans with lighter, easy-to-clean skillets. Adding a slow cooker made it easier to make soups, stews, and casseroles. Reducing the total amount of equipment and utensils in the kitchen made it easier to organize. This makeover allowed the man to keep special and meaningful items while donating the rest. Earlier observations gave them the insight to focus their reorganization on accessibility, usability, and simplicity.

This insight process is iterative. In later design phases, you might need to revisit your empathy data, look at it from a different angle, or even gather more data to check your insights. While collection of empathy data is vital, analysis transforms this data into actionable insights needed for all the following phases of design thinking.

Empathy Maps

Many designers use empathy maps when analyzing empathy data. Empathy maps are handy visual tools that condense the needs of multiple community partners into a concise, easily understood format. They are helpful in identifying patterns and themes for your project and can even reveal if you are asking the right questions.

An empathy map for multiple people makes a composite profile, sometimes called a persona (see the Personas sidebar on page 80). Your empathy map and persona help you understand the perspectives of your community partners better. You can refer to this map when questions arise, and you can revise and refine your persona as you learn more about your community partners.

Creating an Empathy Map

An empathy map is a window into the world of your community partner, segmented into four panels showing what your community partner says, thinks, does, and feels. See the diagrams of a blank map on the next page.

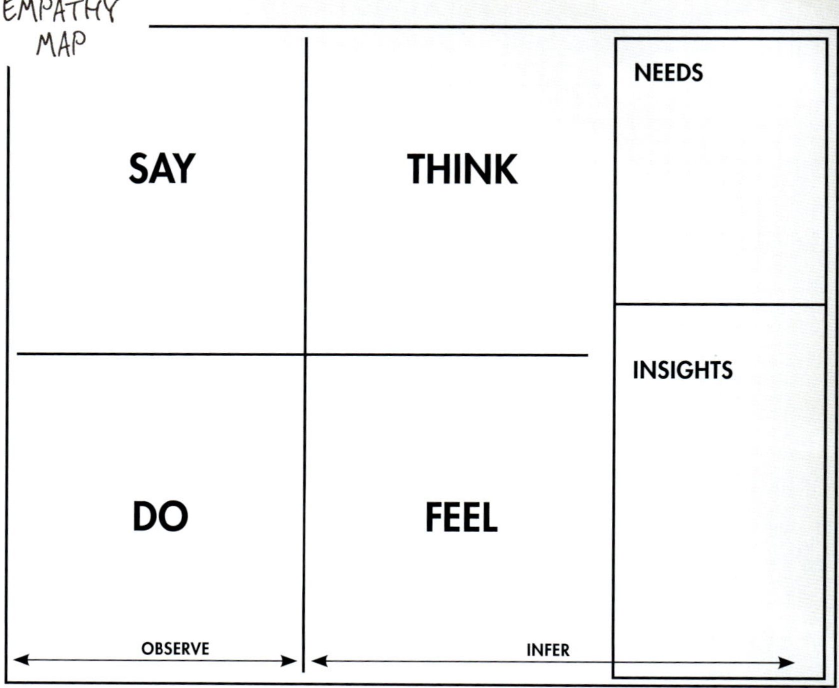

1. **NAME YOUR PERSONA**
   Start by giving your composite community partner—your persona—a face and a name. Add a representative picture and a code name to the center of your empathy map to humanize your data.
2. **FILL OUT "SAY"**
   Fill the "SAY" square with direct quotes from your empathy research. If you paraphrase or summarize, you run their words through your own filters and may unconsciously alter their meaning without noticing it.

   If they express the same issue repeatedly, it could be a significant problem or an important value. Record any challenges, benefits, or expectations your community partner mentions.

3. **FILL OUT "THINK"**

   In the "THINK" square, write the thoughts your community partner expresses in words. Also, note your best guess about how they feel based on their body language, tone, and nonverbal cues during your interview. For example, if a community partner is frowning while describing an event, you might reasonably assume that they have negative feelings about that event.

   But there may be alternative explanations. Your community partner may have been physically uncomfortable if perhaps the interview ran too long, or they may have just remembered an unpleasant task they don't want to do. Check with them.

   This is also a good point to consider if you are making biased assumptions. Be cautious of your assumptions, and ask your community partner for clarification if you are not sure.

4. **FILL OUT "DO"**

   The "DO" square captures your community partner's actions and behaviors. This could include their physical reactions during the interview or how they interact with a device or service they use.

5. **FILL OUT "FEEL"**

   The "FEEL" square reads the emotions of your community partners. They might explicitly express some feelings, or you might infer them from their body language, tone, or expressions. You can ask your community partner "How do you feel about this?" if they don't openly share their thoughts.

As you gather more data, revisit and revise your empathy map. Empathy maps are meant to be updated as research progresses.

Empathy maps live up to their name by helping build empathy with our community partners. They allow us to do the following:

- Remove our biases and align the team with a shared understanding of our community partner
- Identify potential gaps in our research
- Uncover needs that the community partners themselves may not even be aware of
- Understand what drives community partners' behaviors
- Guide us toward meaningful innovation

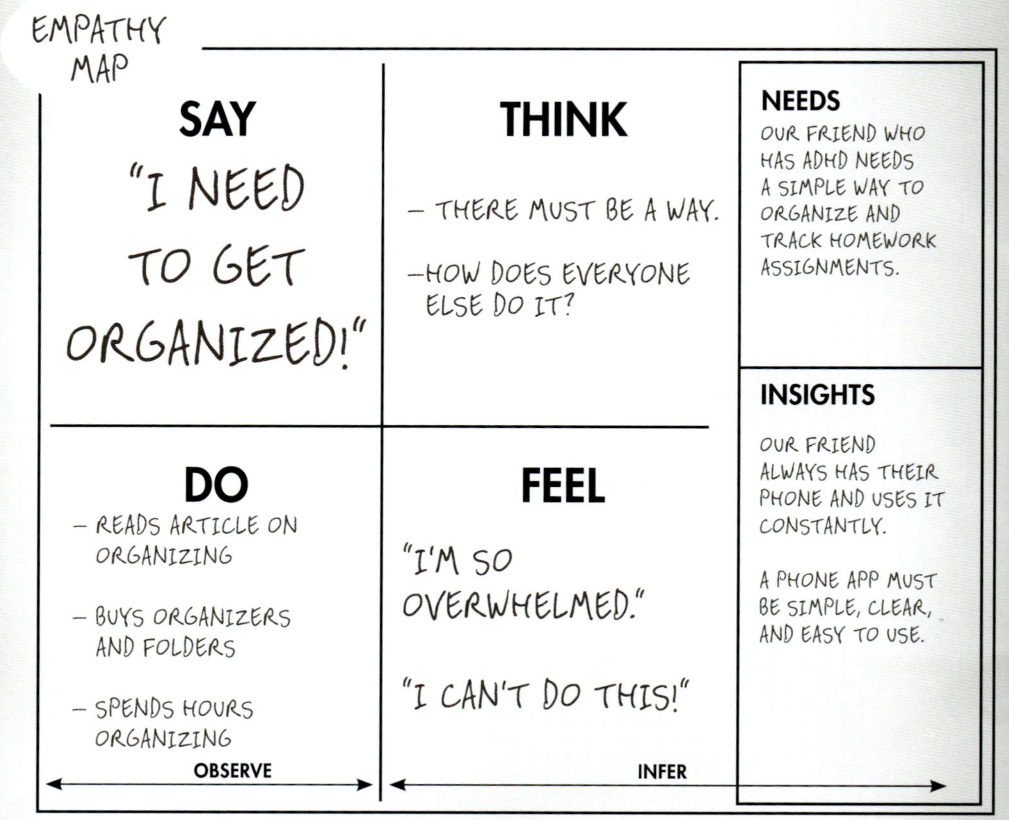

EMPATHY MAP

SAY

"I NEED TO GET ORGANIZED!"

THINK

– THERE MUST BE A WAY.

– HOW DOES EVERYONE ELSE DO IT?

NEEDS

OUR FRIEND WHO HAS ADHD NEEDS A SIMPLE WAY TO ORGANIZE AND TRACK HOMEWORK ASSIGNMENTS.

DO

– READS ARTICLE ON ORGANIZING

– BUYS ORGANIZERS AND FOLDERS

– SPENDS HOURS ORGANIZING

FEEL

"I'M SO OVERWHELMED."

"I CAN'T DO THIS!"

INSIGHTS

OUR FRIEND ALWAYS HAS THEIR PHONE AND USES IT CONSTANTLY.

A PHONE APP MUST BE SIMPLE, CLEAR, AND EASY TO USE.

OBSERVE ⟷ INFER

Empathy Map Example

One team of students described their project to help a classmate with attention deficit hyperactivity disorder (ADHD). Their classmate had trouble staying organized at school and completing their schoolwork. The team wanted to develop a smartphone app to help their friend stay organized. While they did not display an empathy map, it may have looked something like this one in the diagram on page 66. Their empathy map might reveal that their friend feels overwhelmed (FEEL) by the number of assignments. Their friend constantly expressed a need for a better way to manage their workload (SAY). The friend spends a lot of time organizing their tasks (DO), and they wish there were an easier way (THINK).

This pattern could lead to an insight: Students need a feature that helps them remember, organize, and prioritize assignments. From their research and empathy map, the team came to a similar understanding and designed an improved to-do list. It could easily reorder assignments by importance and due date, along with prompts and alarms. Their grateful friend found it much easier to keep up with their work.

Journey Maps

Journey maps depict the story of an individual's interaction with a product, service, or organization over time and across various situations. They illustrate the steps a community partner takes to achieve a goal from start to finish, highlighting key interactions and potential problems along the way.

Sometimes a journey map is the ideal tool to make sense of a community partner's experience. Imagine, for example, a blind person trying to navigate their city's public transportation system. A well-constructed journey map captures the events a community partner encounters during a process, along with their feelings, expectations, and frustrations.

Journey Map (template)

Persona and Goal:

Journey Step					
Feeling/ Emotions					
Feel on scale of 1 to 5					
Thoughts					
Touchpoints					
Opportunities					

These touchpoint events are the various interactions a community partner has with the service or product in use. Journey maps help designers understand and address the needs and challenges of community partners more effectively.

Creating a Journey Map

1. **DEFINE A PERSONA**
   Begin with identifying your composite community partner. In our example, let's call our persona who symbolizes the blind community in urban areas Alicia.
2. **IDENTIFY USER GOALS**
   What is Alicia trying to achieve? Her end goal is independent navigation around the city using public transportation.

Journey Map

Persona and Goal: ALICIA, INDEPENDENT NAVIGATION

JOURNEY STEP	Planning trip	Getting to bus stop	Boarding the bus	Getting off at the right stop	Reaching the right stop
FEELING/ EMOTIONS	Glad to have this app but it could be more intuitive!	The sun feels good, nice day for a short walk, and Rex needs to stretch his legs.	Glad it's a kneeling bus, but I feel everyone watching.	Will driver remember to announce my stop? Hope no one tries to distract Rex.	So glad driver remembered to let me know of the stop in advance.
FEEL ON SCALE OF 1 TO 5	5 4 (3) 2 1	(5) 4 3 2 1	5 4 (3) 2 1	5 4 3 2 (1)	5 (4) 3 2 1
THOUGHTS	Ah, finally, here's the bus I want!	Nice to have this bus stop so close	Remember to wait until kneeling mechanism stops	Was that my stop we just passed?	Here at last!
TOUCHPOINTS	Using an app with bus schedule made for people with limited vision	Sidewalk in good repair with curb cuts	Boarding a kneeling bus	Riding the bus	Disembarking a kneeling bus
OPPORTUNITIES	*Make app more intuitive			*Add destination to the app	

3. **OUTLINE YOUR COMMUNITY PARTNER'S STEPS**
   Break down Alicia's journey into high-level stages such as planning the route, getting to the bus stop, boarding the bus, getting off at the right stop, and reaching the final destination.
4. **DETAIL TOUCHPOINTS**
   List specific interactions Alicia has within each step. This could include using a navigation app, asking passersby for help, locating the bus door, and recognizing her stop.

5. **IDENTIFY EMOTIONS**
   Try to identify Alicia's feelings at each touchpoint. For example, she may feel frustrated when the navigation app isn't accurate or relieved when a passerby offers accurate directions.
6. **HIGHLIGHT OPPORTUNITIES**
   Look for areas of improvement or potential for innovation. Maybe the bus could have audio announcements for each stop or the navigation app could provide more detailed voice instructions for the visually impaired.
7. **VISUALIZE THE JOURNEY**
   Turn Alicia's journey map into a visual document. Use colors and symbols to highlight distinct elements of the journey. A simple chart or a more detailed infographic could work.

A journey map is a living document. As you learn more about your community partner and their journey, refine your map to better reflect their experiences.

Before You Move On

Each technique introduced in this chapter, whether it's for collecting information or making sense of it, is valuable in the Empathize phase of design thinking. Used individually, they can yield important insights. Used in combination, they can amplify the depth and richness of our understanding.

The patterns you discover and the insights you generate form the basis for the Define and Ideate phases—the next phases in the design process. Each insight you uncover is a step toward a better design that truly resonates with your community partners.

Case Study: Embrace Infant Warmer

The journey began as an assignment at Stanford: Design a cost-effective baby incubator for the developing world. A baby incubator is a special enclosed crib that helps newborns, especially low-birth weight babies, maintain a stable environment with controlled temperature and humidity. It supports their growth and protects them from infections and sensory overload until they are strong enough to thrive outside the incubator.

But instead of approaching the challenge from a purely medical or technical standpoint, one student team took an empathetic approach, looking at it through the eyes of those who mattered most: the mothers and babies.

In Nepal the vast number of premature births occur in remote villages, so the team traveled to the capital city of Kathmandu. Their research in these communities revealed that many premature babies born in rural areas never made it to city hospitals. Traditional incubators, with their hefty $20,000 price tag, remained inaccessible to most villagers. Even in the city hospital, donated incubators often proved too complex for local medical staff to operate and maintain. The team realized the true challenge wasn't just creating a cheaper incubator, but an incubator designed for this community and this rugged, remote environment.

Their empathy insights led to the creation of the Embrace Infant Warmer. Resembling a sleeping bag, it wrapped snugly around an infant. The design's genius lay in its phase-change material pouch: a high-tech material which, when heated, could maintain the right temperature for hours without electricity. Recharging the pouch was as simple as boiling it in water for a few minutes. The design was easy to use and fit perfectly with the kangaroo care practice, where

A newborn snuggled in the Embrace Infant Warmer

mothers maintain skin-to-skin contact with their babies to keep the babies warm and bond with them.

The Embrace Infant Warmer, priced at $25, transformed neonatal care in regions where traditional incubators were out of reach, making a significant difference for infants and their families.

The original Stanford student team still runs the company they started, Embrace Global, and gives away one of their original warmers in a developing country for every one of their products they sell in the United States. They estimate that the Embrace Infant Warmer has saved over 475,000 lives.

Empathize Checklist

- ⬡ Have you prepared for your empathy data gathering?
- ⬡ Have you collected enough data from your community partners and stakeholders?
- ⬡ Have you conducted one or more sessions and documented them?
- ⬡ Have you analyzed your empathy data and distilled enough insights for the Define phase?
- ⬡ Have you reflected on the data, validated it with your community partners, and shared it with your team and stakeholders?

Reflection Questions

- How might your personal identity, background, and values shape the way you observe or influence the questions you choose to ask during empathy research?
- In what ways is the role of a design thinker similar to that of a reporter or detective? In what ways is it distinct?
- How does the Empathize phase differ from standard demographic research?
- Beyond traditional observation and interviews, how might internet research enhance and expand your understanding during the Empathize phase?

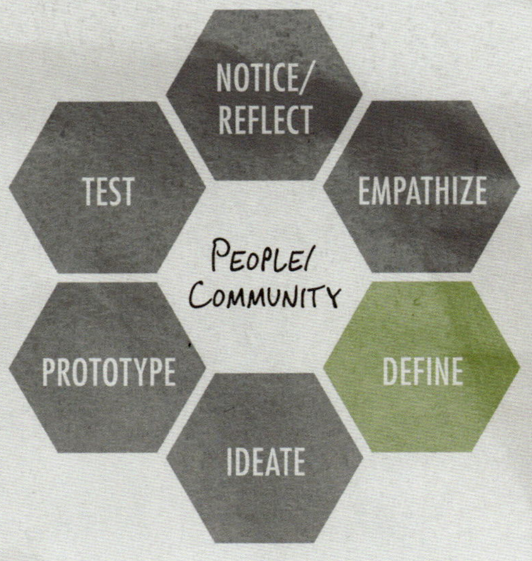

CHAPTER 3
Define

If the ladder is not leaning against the right wall, every step we take just gets us to the wrong place faster.

—STEPHEN COVEY

The Define phase of design thinking combines the insights collected during the Empathize phase and uses a five-step process to condense them into a clear and actionable explanation of the design challenge. The focus of the Define phase is on framing problems around people, rather than just listing issues. These are the five steps:

- Organize and make sense of the empathy data.
- Frame a Problem Statement from the data.
- Ask a "How might we . . ." (HMW) Question based on the Problem Statement.
- Crystalize a Needs Statement for your community partner.
- Synthesize a Point of View (POV) Statement to guide ideation.

Why Is Defining So Important?

The Define phase clarifies insights from the Empathize phase to express the needs of the community partner in simple, direct, actionable language. Like a compass, the Define phase keeps the design team on the right path.

By framing the problem from the perspective of the community partners, designers ensure solutions are tailored to real human needs and feelings. When we prioritize people first, we create better solutions.

A well-defined problem provides a sharp focus to ensure we direct our efforts toward the exact issue that needs addressing. The team does not waste its efforts on solving the wrong problem and increases the chances of a successful outcome.

When everyone in the team understands the challenge in the same way, it sets a common ground for collaboration. The team can also more easily communicate a well-defined problem with community partners and potential supporters.

With a well-defined challenge, the team knows their goal and the criteria for success. Also, it's easier to gather relevant feedback during prototyping and testing phases.

Work through this phase thoughtfully. Then your team can move faster and with more confidence during the rest of the process.

You Are Here in the Design Thinking Process

At the end of the Empathize phase, the design team has gathered a great deal of information from the community partners about their problem and about how the problem affects their lives. The Define phase consolidates and condenses this information into a clear expression of what community partners want.

In this chapter, we see Team Squggle members Avery and Lilli take their holistic understanding of community partners Chiara and Elena's situation to work through the five steps of the Define phase. The final step, the POV Statement, will guide the next phase of the design process.

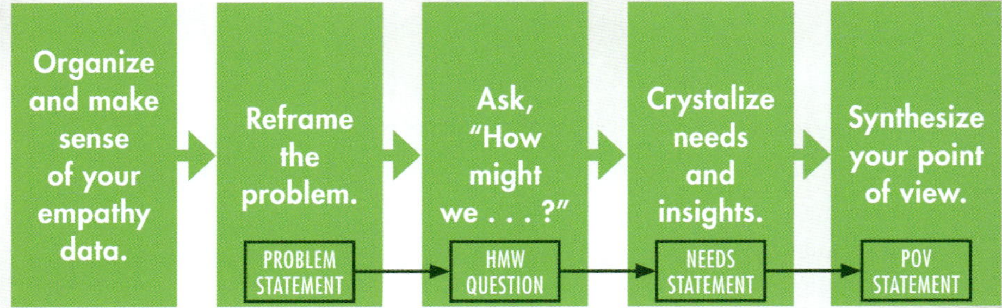

In this chapter, you'll find how to transform your empathetic research into actionable insights that will direct the Ideate phase, while always considering diverse perspectives. Specifically, you'll learn how to

- Apply the five-step Define phase model to your project
- Deepen your empathy by **synthesizing** your research data and identifying **theme** patterns
- Create and use journey maps and personas to visually experience and identify problems
- Use Notice and Reflect phase questions to avoid **groupthink**
- Follow the progression of the statements and learn how the POV Statement will guide the Ideate phase

Troubleshooting Define Phase Challenges

Size of Dataset

CHALLENGE

You collect an overwhelming amount of data during the empathy phase.

SOLUTION

Consolidate data by categorizing and tagging the information to see patterns. See how on pages 79–80.

Not Specific Enough

CHALLENGE

Your problem statements are vague.

SOLUTION

Revisit the tagged empathy data to ensure the focus is on community partners and their issues.

Biased Thinking

CHALLENGE

Your team struggles with groupthink assumptions and bias. If group members focus more on agreeing and getting along than on examining ideas critically, they may quickly settle on mistaken assumptions or understandings. This limits creativity and innovation and may even allow bias to creep in.

SOLUTION

Review the Notice and Reflect phase questions, and always encourage the team to challenge assumptions.

Complexity

CHALLENGE

You face very complex problems that resist definition.

SOLUTION

Break down larger problems into smaller, more manageable parts. Tackle each part individually before piecing them together.

Clarity of Purpose

CHALLENGE

The problem is too abstract.

SOLUTION

Always tie the problem's definition statements back to the stories of your community partners. Create personas and journey maps to sharpen the focus on your community partners and their experience with the problem.

Case Study: Team Squggle

Chiara, a nine-year-old girl, has cerebral palsy with quadriplegia, so she cannot move her arms or legs, and she is nonverbal. Usually confined to her bed, she and her mom communicate in their own special language of expressions, gestures, and sounds.

Her mother, Elena, is home with her, offering love and care. But sometimes Elena, who works from home, must work in another room. For safety and peace of mind, they both want a way for Chiara to signal for her mom when needed. Elena is also interested in ways to comfort, entertain, and interest Chiara when they are not together.

Avery and Lilli chose to help Elena and Chiara with these challenges as their design project. During their Empathize phase, they learned about the lives of Chiara and Elena, their home situation, and the profound bond between mother and daughter. They saw a family striving to connect, a mother trying to provide comfort and engagement for her daughter, and a young girl longing to stay in contact with her mother.

Remembering the quip about ensuring the ladder is against the right wall before climbing, they defined their question carefully. "How might we enable Chiara to communicate with her mother, ensuring her safety and well-being, while also enriching her world and offering stimulating and absorbing experiences?" With this clearly articulated challenge, Avery and Lilli moved to the next steps of their design project.

Steps in Define Phase

1. ORGANIZE AND MAKE SENSE OF THE EMPATHY DATA

During the Empathize phase, you gathered piles of data: interview notes, bits of conversation, photos, and maybe some voice notes of your observations. All this vital information can be difficult to make sense of in isolation.

Just as you would look for edge pieces and start grouping images of a puzzle, you can organize your empathy data to find patterns and connections. When you process this information, you see the underlying problems and any hidden challenges.

As you go through the information you've gathered, you'll notice recurring ideas, themes, feelings, or issues. Use highlighting tools to mark these repeating elements. Color coding recurrent ideas helps you visualize the patterns in, and frequency of, concepts.

Once you identify patterns, categorize these data into groups to identify larger themes. Here, the creation of personas can be particularly useful. By synthesizing this categorized data, you can develop detailed personas that represent different segments of your community partners and stakeholders, providing a foundation for understanding their needs, behaviors, and problems.

Visual aids including mind maps and journey maps can help you organize the information too. A mind map is a diagram used to organize information visually. Similarly, a journey map offers a visual representation of your community partner's experience with a problem or situation. It showcases their interactions, emotions, and problems throughout their interaction.

Creating a journey map, as shown in the Empathize chapter, can help identify areas of opportunity and

Personas

What Is a Persona?

A persona is a made-up character representing a segment of your community partners or stakeholders. Personas embody the characteristics, needs, and goals of a larger group. For instance, Team Alertra might create a persona for someone hard of hearing to guide their design for a fire alarm watch.

But teams with specific partners, such as Team Syphon's Deyon and Jomari, might initially skip this step, then revisit it if they decide to commercialize their device to represent broader client types.

Why Use Personas?

Personas are a major tool in design thinking. They focus the design work firmly on the community partner to ensure that solutions closely align with their genuine needs. By humanizing this data, personas foster a deeper connection to community partner experiences and can lead to more empathetic and effective solutions.

uncover insights into the needs and challenges your community partners face. These visual tools, along with the developed personas, will aid in revealing the hidden challenges and stories within your empathy data. They set the stage for framing the problem statement in the next step of the Define phase.

2. **FRAME THE PROBLEM STATEMENT FOR THE DATA**

   A Problem Statement describes the challenge or problem faced by the community partners without prescribing a solution. Problem Statements are usually broad and help the design team understand the fundamental challenge in terms of what the community partner wants to accomplish.

How to Create a Persona

1. **Conduct research and identify patterns.** Gather both qualitative and quantitative data through interviews, surveys, and observations to understand the needs, behaviors, and characteristics of your community partners. Analyze this data to uncover common patterns and themes.
2. **Define segments.** Based on the identified patterns, segment the community partners into groups with similar characteristics to form the basis for each persona.
3. **Develop detailed personas.** For each segment, craft a detailed persona, incorporating demographics, behaviors, needs, goals, problems, and scenarios.
4. **Personalize the persona.** Bring each persona to life with a name, face, and backstory to enhance relatability.
5. **Validate and refine.** Validate the personas with additional research and stakeholder input, refining them as needed to ensure accuracy in representing the community partner base.
6. **Share and reference.** Distribute the completed personas to the team and stakeholders, using them as a regular reference to guide decision-making and maintain a community partner focus.

For example, “When Elena is in another room, she cannot know when Chiara needs help or attention,” states the core issue clearly, without suggesting a solution. An alternative Problem Statement from the viewpoint of the other community partner could be “Chiara, because of her cerebral palsy, cannot communicate her needs when her mother, Elena, is in another room.”

The statement “Elena needs a video monitoring system to better care for Chiara” describes a particular solution, so it is not a good Problem Statement. If we describe a need as a noun (a thing), rather than as a verb (an action), it may require more thinking. Nouns often signal an implied

Alternative Communication Vocalization

Alternative communication vocalizations are sounds produced by the vocal cords that are used to communicate. People who cannot speak due to a variety of medical conditions, such as cerebral palsy or stroke, use them to express needs, thoughts, and feelings to caregivers. This is how Chiara and Elena communicate.

Cerebral palsy is a group of neurological disorders that affect movement, coordination, speech, and other functioning. It is caused by damage to the developing brain before or during birth. Cerebral palsy can affect speech and communication in a variety of ways. Some people with cerebral palsy may have difficulty articulating words, while others may have difficulty speaking clearly, and others may not speak at all.

Alternative communication vocalizations can help people with cerebral palsy communicate with their caregivers more effectively. For example, a person with cerebral palsy might use a crying sound to express hunger or a coo to express happiness. A caregiver can learn to interpret these vocalizations and respond accordingly.

There are many benefits to using alternative communication vocalizations for people with cerebral palsy and their caregivers. For people with cerebral palsy, alternative communication vocalizations can help them gain more independence and to engage more fully with others. For caregivers, alternative communication vocalizations can help them better understand and meet the needs of their loved ones. For both, vocalizations can reduce stress and frustration.

Alternative communication vocalizations are an important tool for people with cerebral palsy and their caregivers. Future research may help develop new technology, techniques, and support programs for caregivers.

solution, while verbs generally show what your community partner is trying to achieve.

"Elena wants to improve her home for Chiara" is an example of a vague Problem Statement. It is unclear because it doesn't define what "improve" means in this context. Does it refer to making the home more accessible? More stimulating? Safer? Without specifics, the design team won't know where to focus their efforts. A clear and concise Problem Statement provides direction and focus to the design team and helps keep the design effort on track.

Lilli and Avery avoided a quick, preconceived Problem Statement and could then design a better solution for Chiara and Elena. They preserved the possibility of finding a more comprehensive solution that filled more of the needs Chiara described.

3. ASK A "HOW MIGHT WE . . . ?" QUESTION BASED ON THE PROBLEM STATEMENT

After you have framed a good Problem Statement, turn it into a question with the phrase "How might we . . . ?" This shift encourages creative thinking, which leads to multiple possible solutions.

With no one, single, "right" answer, a "How might we . . . ?" Question is open-ended and nonjudgmental. The HMW Question asks how something *might* be done, rather than how it *should* be done. The "we" in HMW invites everyone's ideas, regardless of their level of experience, expertise, or status.

For example, let's develop the Problem Statement "When Elena is in another room, she cannot know when Chiara needs help or attention" into a HMW Question. It becomes "How might we help Elena know Chiara needs help or attention when Elena is in another room?" Or, using the case of Jomari and Deyon from the Empathize chapter, "How might we help Deyon care for his son and still get enough sleep?"

4. **CREATE A NEEDS STATEMENT FOR YOUR COMMUNITY PARTNER**
While the "How might we . . . ?" Question encourages open-ended problem-solving, its corollary is the Needs Statement, which focuses on the specific requirements of the community partners. It zeroes in on actionable requirements. It encourages team members to look for underlying root causes of problems, to be sure the ladder is leaning against the right wall.
This need is a gap or deficiency in the experience or current situation of your community partners. The base phrase "needs a way to . . ." puts the emphasis on tangible action. For example, "Elena needs a way to know when Chiara requires help or attention," or "Javier needs a way to know when he starts to veer while walking."

5. **SYNTHESIZE A POINT OF VIEW (POV) STATEMENT TO GUIDE IDEATION**
A Point of View Statement combines deep insights about the needs of your community partners with your team's insights or interpretations based on your empathy work. It not only expresses the needs of your community partners but also gives a particular lens or direction for potential solutions. The POV Statement is often a result of synthesizing raw observations and finding meaningful patterns.

Structure of POV Statements

A well-crafted POV Statement often has three key components:

- Your community partners
- The core need of your partners
- Deeper insight based on the Empathize observations

The Five Whys Technique

The "Five Whys" is a technique used primarily for root cause analysis. It involves asking "Why?" repeatedly (typically five times, but it can be more or fewer as needed) to peel away the layers of an issue and get to the root cause of a problem.

By identifying the core issue, one can address the actual cause rather than just the symptoms. The "Five Whys" technique is especially useful in the Define and Empathize phases.

During the Define phase, this technique aids in crafting a clear and accurate Problem Statement. Addressing the real underlying issue (rather than surface-level symptoms) will make the subsequent phases of the design thinking process (Ideate, Prototype, and Test) much more effective.

For example, if Chiara can't communicate when Elena is in another room, you might ask these kinds of questions:

- Why can't Chiara communicate? Chiara can't speak or move.
- Why can't Chiara speak or move? Chiara has a type of cerebral palsy that includes quadriplegia and makes speech nearly impossible.
- Why do those conditions make movement or speech impossible? (And so on . . .)

Here, Lilli and Avery will find out that Chiara has some limited hand movement and can communicate with her mom in a limited way through vocalizations. By the end of this process, they also find the problem isn't just about communication but also involves feelings of independence, safety concerns, and connection. As seen from the example, each answer forms the basis of the next question.

This technique can also be useful during the Empathize phase, when gathering insights and raw data from users. The "Five Whys" can help in understanding the deeper emotions, motivations, and challenges that community partners might be facing. Asking "Why?" five times usually draws out more information with each turn.

Case Study: The Town Pool

In one Scandinavian town, the community swimming pool had always been a hub of activity, and everyone enjoyed it. But in a brief span of time, attendance dropped sharply. The concerned town council jumped to the conclusion that the pool complex had become outdated and believed a new pool was the answer. They selected an architect and invited him to present design concepts for their multimillion-dollar vision.

Yet when the architect arrived at the council meeting, he didn't bring intricate scale models of a proposed pool complex. Instead, he held up a single sheet of paper. The architect explained that he closely inspected the pool and then talked with the people in town, especially frequent swimmers. After these conversations, he realized an outdated pool wasn't leading to poor attendance. The sheet he held up? The town's bus schedule.

One of the town's bus routes ran right by the pool, and most people rode the bus to the pool. But the town's transportation department had recently changed the bus schedule so that the buses only ran along the route to the pool in midmornings and midafternoon. They dropped the early morning and later afternoon runs—the times when most of the daily swimmers went to the pool before or after work. The architect's insight was simple: revert to the old bus timetable.

Taking his advice, the town saw pool attendance rebound to the previous levels and saved time and millions of tax dollars. This architect had done more than solve a problem. He made sure the town

Let's look at each part. By now, just naming your community partners evokes specific people and a specific situation. You refined the core need in your Needs Statement. These needs often represent basic elements that will combine into a solution later in the design process.

Having conversations with community members helps to better understand what issues they really face.

solved the *real* problem. The town learned the value of placing their ladder against the right wall.

Insight doesn't just recognize a need. It digs deeper into the reasons behind that need. Insight touches the emotions, motivations, and underlying factors that drive need. These insights are often "aha" moments when a design team deeply understands the community partners and their experience. Insights can often lead to innovative solutions that might not be immediately obvious from the basic need.

For example, Elena, mother of a daughter needing comprehensive care, experiences anxiety and worry that her daughter may need her, but Elena may not consciously acknowledge it. Chiara, her daughter, feels isolated and dependent because of her inability to move well or to communicate easily. This leads to moments of frustration, loneliness, and sadness. Because of this, the solution should not just address the communications need but also help these feelings of isolation, dependence, and anxiety.

POV Format

An easy format for a POV Statement is this: [Your community partner] needs [add the action-oriented need here] in order to [insight about underlying important emotional satisfaction].

Here's an example: "Elena, a dedicated mother, needs a way to ensure Chiara's safety when she's in another room because she wants to provide both comfort for Chiara, peace of mind for herself, and a feeling of close connection for them both." You can write a POV from the perspective of any community partner. In the case of Elena and Chiara, they differ but complement each other.

With this format, the design team focuses on the core problem while creating a compelling narrative for the Ideate phase.

Before You Move On

This chapter guided you through the systematic process of defining the design project for a community partner.

The culmination of the Define phase is a well-constructed POV Statement free of implied solutions and verified by the community partner. This concise and actionable statement guides the Ideate phase and helps the team decide when they have achieved a satisfactory solution.

For example, a reader of this book needs a clear explanation of the Define phase of design thinking to create useful definitions of design problems and to feel the satisfaction of improving people's lives.

Define Checklist

- ⬡ Is your empathy data organized into thematic patterns with personas, diagrams, mind maps, and journey maps?
- ⬡ Have you completed all the steps and statements in the Define phase?
- ⬡ Have you verified the Needs and POV Statements with your community partner?
- ⬡ Have you documented and backed up the important learnings and insights from this phase?

Reflection Questions

- Is it clear how to move from a Problem Statement through a HMW and a Needs Statement to a POV Statement?
- How would you write a Needs Statement for the community partners of the Oakland middle school students and their neighborhood park?
- How would you explain to a teammate the value of going through each step separately rather than just skipping directly from the data analysis to a Point of View Statement?
- Can you recall any situations when jumping to conclusions without understanding the root cause of a problem resulted in a big mistake? Or, like the Scandinavian town pool, when did people avoid a big mistake by identifying the root cause?

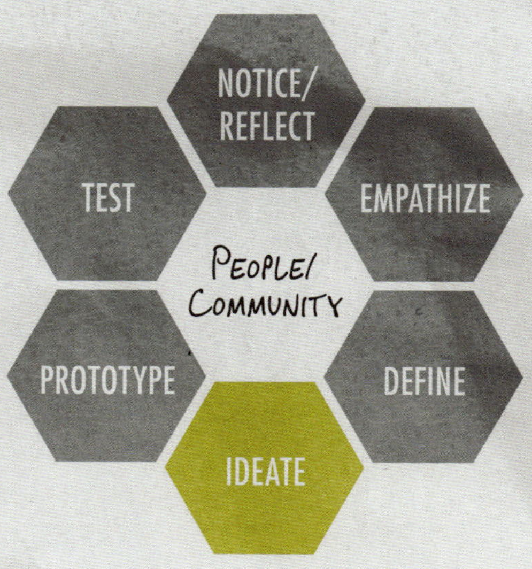

CHAPTER 4

Ideate

**If you always do what you have always done,
you will always get what you always got.**

—HENRY FORD

It is easier to tone down a wild idea than to think up a new one.

—ATTRIBUTED TO ALEX OSBORN

Ideation, when paired with observation, is a transformative problem-solving tool. Team Syphon and Team Alertra discovered its potential in directing a group's creative energies toward generating fresh ideas and approaches.

While often used interchangeably with "brainstorming," ideation is a broader concept. Beyond brainstorming, it includes methods of grouping and prioritizing the ideas produced. While people in fields such as marketing and engineering sometimes use this term, "ideation" in design thinking stresses creativity, innovation, and

significant change. Through a more complete ideation process, you expand potential solutions and then focus on the most promising ones for prototyping.

Why Is Ideation So Important?

Design thinking builds ideation into its process to explore different solutions and choose the best ones, rather than going with the first or most obvious solution. After all, if there were a simple answer or a proven formula, you would not need design thinking.

For example, math problems may be difficult to solve until you find the right formula. Then you get the right answer every time. But figuring out which career path to follow is complex, personal, and involves many factors. Design thinking excels at complex problems such as career planning. (By the way, I list *Designing Your Life*, an excellent book on applying design thinking to your personal decisions, in the Going Further section.)

The Ideate phase of design thinking helps improve problem-solving in these ways:

- Exploring a range of choices
- Encouraging wild and creative ideas to find new and better options
- Generating dramatically different solutions, not simply minor changes to the status quo
- Deepening the team's understanding of the problem

For example, a group such as Team Alertra might brainstorm how to improve firefighter safety at a fire. But they would quickly realize that many types of solutions were too expensive, take too long, or require specialized training. Realizing this, the team could go back to redefining the Needs Statement. They might even go back to their empathy research to check their understanding of the people, purpose, and context. Although these revisions may take more time, they ensure that the solution will truly fix the problem for the community partners.

You Are Here in the Design Thinking Process

Now that you have defined the problem of your community partners and completed a Needs Statement, you are ready to get creative with the Ideate phase.

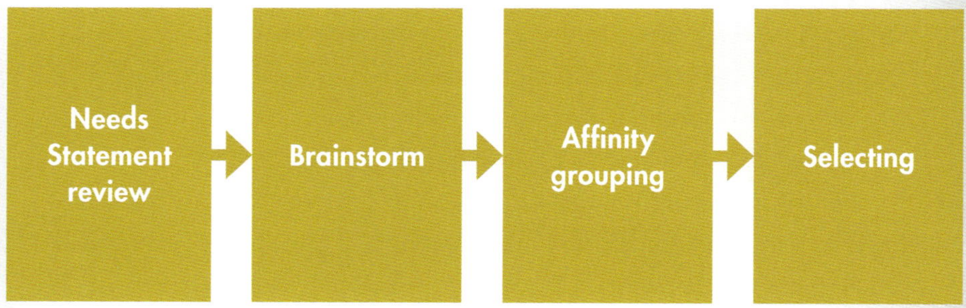

In this chapter, you'll explore and apply the three integral and interlocking steps of ideation—brainstorming, affinity grouping, and selecting—to effectively generate and refine ideas. Specifically, you'll learn how to

- Apply the three components of ideation
- Conduct a productive brainstorming session
- Harness affinity grouping to organize your ideas
- Select a few promising concepts for prototyping
- Work with ideation guidelines and several simple decision tools

Steps in Ideate Phase

The ideation method was developed from the technique of brainstorming devised by advertising executive Alex Osborn. There are four major steps to the ideation process:

1. **REVIEW THE NEEDS STATEMENT**

   Begin your ideation session with a brief review of the Needs Statement developed with your community

partners. This review will remind everyone of the goal of this session. The team may also realize the Needs Statement requires some adjustment.

2. **BRAINSTORM**

During brainstorming, the team generates many potential solutions for the problem in a short time. Encourage divergent, innovative, and even wild ideas. At the end of the brainstorming phase, the team will have a long list of possibilities to investigate.

To set the right tone, kick off the session with some creativity warm-ups to help people feel comfortable and get ideas flowing. For example, in one classic warm-up, the group lists as many ideas as they can think of in three minutes for how to use a brick. Encourage people to think "out of the box" and go for as many ideas as possible. You can give the example that using bricks to build a fireplace or to line a walk are fine suggestions and to begin their list with these more commonplace applications.

Then invite people to experiment with something more unusual or sillier. For example, someone might propose grinding up a brick and using the powder to make paint or a dye for cloth. These creativity exercises help people move beyond seeing things only in an everyday context. The Going Further section lists more creativity-spurring activities.

In the most familiar and popular method of brainstorming, the team works with sticky notes around a table with a large whiteboard nearby. After the initial warm-up, everyone writes as many ideas for a solution or a part of a solution as they can think up.

Each sticky note should have only one idea. This way, the writing is more legible, and it will be easier to regroup

Students write down ideas (one per note) during a brainstorming session.

the notes later. If everyone adds their initials to their sticky notes, the author can later elaborate on a vague or unclear message. When I'm trying to get ideas down quickly during brainstorming, my difficult-to-read handwriting deteriorates even further. Remind everyone to go for quantity and to not hold themselves back.

After an initial burst of activity, people may slow down. You might call out some encouragement. You could also note a part of the Needs Statement not yet addressed.

Once you feel the team has expressed all their ideas, everyone can begin putting their sticky notes on the whiteboard for all to see. As the stickies go on the board, you might read some of the suggestions out loud. This often spurs a fresh round of thoughts from team members. Add these as new sticky notes to the board.

Sometimes a new idea emerges that links to an existing idea on the board. Other times, the new sticky note is a variation of an existing idea or something extending that idea. Keep in mind, the goal of this brainstorming step is to get as many ideas as possible.

Celebrate unconventional ideas. Research on creativity shows that odd or quirky ideas may lead to trailblazing solutions. Many revolutionary innovations seemed silly to people at first. After all, in 1976 when Apple cofounders Steve Jobs and Steve Wozniak began selling the personal computers that they built in a garage, the so-called experts on computers at that time dismissed these personal computers as impractical toys.

When the group has posted all the ideas it can generate in this session on the board, start organizing and clarifying these ideas.

Post notes on a wall or whiteboard. At this stage, it's OK to go for quantity!

Troubleshooting Brainstorming Challenges

Team Hesitation

CHALLENGE

Team members hesitate to share ideas.

SOLUTION

Encourage every voice. Remind everyone that each team member brings a unique perspective.

Criticizing Creativity

CHALLENGE

Criticisms come up during brainstorming.

SOLUTION

Remind everyone that brainstorming is a no-judgment zone. Judgment dampens creativity.

Jumping to Adopt the First Idea

CHALLENGE

The team rushes to adopt the first idea.

SOLUTION

Highlight the value of iteration and why it's important to revisit and improve ideas. Taking your time now can speed up the process later.

Convergent Ideas

CHALLENGE

There's a lack of divergent thinking.

SOLUTION

Generate a wide range of ideas before converging on selected solutions. Divergent thinking fuels creativity and innovation.

Negative Attitude

CHALLENGE

Team members offer negative feedback without solid evidence.

SOLUTION

Invite feedback and seek advice but trust your intuition. Pay close attention to the community partners. People who offer constructive feedback with supporting reasons often have a good point. People who flatly say an idea won't work without justifying their claim are often missing the point.

3. CLUSTER AFFINITIES

Sort all the sticky note ideas into related groups known as affinity clusters. By grouping similar ideas together, the design team can zero in on the top ones that really stand out. This makes it far easier to pick the best ideas to bring to life through prototyping.

Ask the team to look for similar ideas and cluster them together. Don't toss out ones that are just a bit different since that difference may become important later. Simply put those stickies close together.

Don't reject ideas that don't seem to belong with any cluster. These outliers may seem off topic, odd, impractical, or too big. Set these to the side. Later on, if searching for an alternative approach, these outliers may contain the glimmer of a new line of thought.

If people feel that an idea belongs in two or more clusters, simply copy that idea onto a new sticky note so that it can be in more than one group. This clustering is also a thinking and reflecting step. Don't be surprised if the room's energy level and excitement spikes during this stage, as often happens in my sessions.

Aim for clarity as you summarize and refine these ideas. Your team can then focus on a few key categories and examine the interrelationships. Your team can also combine and mesh ideas, fill in "blank spaces," and even add new ideas inspired by these groupings.

4. **LABEL AFFINITY CLUSTERS**

After grouping the sticky notes, look at each cluster. What would you name this concept or theme? What would be its hashtag? Label each cluster with a bigger note or a bright color. For instance, we might label one cluster "wearable monitor" and another "process redesign."

Most often, teams are amazed to realize that there are so many directions they could take. If you're ever stuck and feel as if you need more inspiration, there are tools and techniques such as SCAMPER, which stands for Substitute, Combine, Adjust, Modify, Put to other uses, Eliminate, Reverse. For more on SCAMPER, see the sidebar on page 101.

Labeling idea clusters highlights the themes of the ideation session.

Case Study: Creativity Research Shows "Go for Quantity"

Can your frame of mind affect your creative abilities? The research of Stanford psychology professor Carol Dweck on fixed and growth mindsets shows it does.

Someone with a fixed mindset believes abilities and intelligence are static and unchangeable, leading them to avoid challenges to avoid failure. In contrast, a growth mindset embraces challenges, seeing them as opportunities to learn and grow. This mindset asserts that people can develop their abilities with effort, practice, and perseverance.

Jerry Uelsmann, then an art professor at the University of Florida, once conducted an experiment on creativity with his novice photography students. He told one section of his class that their grade would depend only on the quality of a single photo they would submit by the semester's end. He challenged the other section to take as many photos as possible. Their grade would be based on quantity, not quality.

At the end of the semester, expert photographers evaluated the students' work. The Quantity group produced the most striking photos. During follow-up with his students, Uelsmann learned that the Quality section took very few photos and were concerned about taking perfect pictures. In focusing on perfection, they were less willing to try new things. The Quantity section used their opportunity to explore and be creative as they took stacks of photos. They experimented with light, camera angles, composition, filters, lenses, and subject matter. In doing this, they pushed their skills and didn't agonize about trying to be perfect. Free to tap the full scope of their imaginations, they learned more and produced better photos.

Uelsmann realized he had instilled a perfectionistic, fixed mindset in the Quality group. But he had encouraged a freewheeling growth mindset in the Quantity group. Applying his own research, Uelsmann then encouraged all his students to embrace experimentation and to focus on learning, rather than perfection.

5. **CLARIFY CONCEPTS**

Once the affinity clusters seem stable, evaluate them. Is the concept in each cluster clear enough for action? Which clusters seem most likely to fix the problem defined in the Needs Statement?

For example, in the Define chapter, we developed Needs Statements for Javier and Elena. "Javier needs a way to know when he starts to veer while walking," and "Elena needs a way to know when Chiara requires help or attention."

With the clusters in focus, the team should refine them. Begin by clarifying, summarizing, and simplifying each group into an explicit solution statement.

Using the examples above, solution statements might be "a wearable belt that vibrates when Javier veers" and "a stuffed animal comfort companion that alerts Elena when Chiara needs attention." With all these promising options, you and the team can decide which ones to pursue.

6. **SELECT POTENTIAL SOLUTIONS TO PROTOTYPE**

With your ideas clustered and summarized, you will have many potential solutions to choose from. To whittle these down, first establish your selection criteria. Primarily, you're aiming for solutions that align with the Needs Statement and fit within your available resources. Refreshing your memory of the Needs Statement can aid this step.

As you assess each option, consider factors such as cost, time frame, scope, and team capabilities. Questions such as "Is it within budget?" and "How long will it take to implement?" and "Does it match our skills?" are crucial. The most important question is "Will this solution delight our community partners?" List these criteria on the whiteboard.

SCAMPER

The SCAMPER technique is a creative problem-solving tool that can generate new ideas or improve existing products, services, or processes. Developed by Alex Osborn, the creator of brainstorming, it was refined by noted creativity coach Bob Eberle. The technique involves asking seven different questions, each represented by a letter in the acronym SCAMPER:

1. **Substitute.** What elements of the current solution can be replaced with something else? Substitution can help to identify alternatives that may be more efficient, effective, or innovative.
2. **Combine.** How can different elements of the solution be brought together or merged? Combining elements can lead to synergistic effects and the creation of something new.
3. **Adapt.** How can the current solution be adjusted or changed to serve a new purpose or function? Adapting a solution can help to extend its utility or reach a broader audience.
4. **Modify, minify, and magnify.** What attributes of the solution can be altered or adjusted? Modification can enhance the solution's appeal, functionality, or impact.
5. **Put to other uses.** In what other contexts or applications could the current solution be used? Repurposing a solution can open up new markets or solve additional problems.
6. **Eliminate.** What elements of the current solution can be removed or simplified? Elimination can lead to a more streamlined and efficient solution.
7. **Rearrange or reverse.** How can the order or orientation of the elements be changed? Rearranging or reversing elements can lead to new insights and perspectives.

When applying the SCAMPER technique, be open to a wide range of possibilities and to encourage divergent thinking. You can use the technique in brainstorming sessions, in design sprints, or as a solo exercise. By systematically exploring these different approaches, teams can uncover novel ideas and innovative solutions.

Case Study: Team Alertra

The affinity clustering phase of brainstorming is a blend of breaking ideas down into simpler parts and then piecing them back together into a better idea. Team Alertra provides a real-world example of this analysis and synthesis process. This team partnered with the Leary Firefighters Foundation of New York City to find ways to safeguard firefighters in action.

After empathy interviews with firefighters Fred and Adam, Team Alertra thought, "Why not keep firefighters safe by minimizing their time inside burning buildings?" They learned that searching for deaf or hard-of-hearing individuals who might be unaware of the fire is critical—it is literally a matter of life or death. These individuals often don't hear the alarm, and sound sleepers may not see flames or smell smoke until it is too late to make a safe escape. Yet these searches can take a lot of time, especially at night in a smoke-filled building. What if the team designed a device that could quickly alert these individuals to danger so they could evacuate promptly without the assistance of others?

Their brainstorming produced a flood of ideas—way too many to prototype. After affinity clustering, they had narrowed them to several practical ideas. During this process, for example, they might have labeled their affinity clusters as "wearable vibrating sensor," "sensor that flashes lights," "sensor that makes a bed shake," or even "sensor that places a call to emergency services."

Next, it's time to zero in on one or a couple of ideas to prototype. One simple approach is to discuss and choose as a group, while keeping the focus on the decision criteria. While some choices might be obvious to the group, it's vital to ensure the team hears every voice and does not sideline disagreements or alternative

Team Alertra shows their invention at Demo Day.

Then, after some productive debates, the team decided to start with the wearable vibrating sensor cluster. They planned to add more complex features, such as the emergency call function, later on. One team member perfectly summed up their journey by likening it to a funnel. "At first, during our brainstorming, it's like the wide end of a funnel where we're pouring in all these ideas. As time goes on, we move deeper into the funnel, weeding out ideas that aren't practical or exceed our budget. And finally, at the funnel's narrowest point, we find our final idea, our best idea."

suggestions too hastily. Ask yourselves, "Which solutions seem the most promising? Which are we most excited to prototype?"

Another popular method involves using colored sticky dots for voting. Give each team member three dots to allocate among their favorite ideas. Before voting, take a moment to reflect on the decision criteria to avoid the trap of groupthink. That's when group members conform to a consensus opinion rather than critically evaluating alternative viewpoints. Discussions or campaigning for a particular choice should not take place during voting.

How many dots should you give everyone? A good guideline is no more dots than a quarter of the total number of choices. Too many can lead to decision paralysis. People will ask if they can place all their dots on a single choice. As facilitator, you decide if this will work well with this group. Digital tools listed in Going Further can also facilitate this selection process.

For close choices with many criteria, analytically inclined groups can use the weight-and-rate method. Here, the group assigns numerical weights to each decision criterion based on its importance, then scores each idea cluster accordingly. The idea with the highest cumulative score emerges as the top pick. See the sidebar on pages 106 and 107 for a more detailed explanation of this method.

By the end of this process, you will have selected a few ideas for prototyping that best fit the needs of your community partners.

Getting Set for Ideation Work

Size

What is the right size for an ideation group? Both the research consensus and my own personal experience suggest about five people as the best size. You can adjust this by one or two people, depending on the specific situation. A group smaller than three might miss diverse or necessary viewpoints, while a group larger than seven often loses focus, leading to phone checking and side conversations. Find a balance

that ensures vibrant discussion, stimulates fresh ideas, and encourages hearing every voice.

Participants

Your design team should naturally be a part of the ideation process. But if key members of the community facing the problem aren't already on your team, it's crucial to include them. Ensure everyone present understands the issue at hand, commits to finding a solution, and actively contributes as a problem solver. Aim for a group that represents all vital community viewpoints without being too big. Keep in mind your commitment from the Notice and Reflect phase to an inclusive and human-centered approach. Are any key viewpoints or groups excluded? Might there be unintended social impacts? Is the group oriented toward human-centered ethics and respect? Meeting these standards confirm your team is living by its values.

Scheduling

Think about the timing. Avoid scheduling sessions when participants are likely to be distracted or have scheduling conflicts. Few people are at their best on Friday afternoons or early on Monday mornings. Aim for a slot when everyone can be present, attentive, and unhurried.

Facilities

Choose a pleasant workspace for ideation. Look for an uncluttered room with good lighting, a comfortable temperature, and a space for snacks and water. Tables and chairs should be movable to accommodate flexible group discussion seating arrangements. Whiteboards or chart paper are essential for visualizing ideas. Ample wall space for hanging chart paper also helps.

Most organizations have meeting spaces like this. If your organization lacks a suitable space, consider reaching out to community

The Weight-and-Rate Decision Method

The weight-and-rate method, also called a weighted decision matrix, is a technique to help you make choices when you have several options. You use it by comparing the options based on specific criteria that matter to you and assigning scores to each option. Here's how to do it:

1. **List the options.** Write down all the options you're considering.
2. **Identify the criteria.** Decide on the factors that are important for your decision. These could include things like cost, time, fun, or any other factors that matter to you.
3. **Assign weights to criteria.** Give a numbered score—a weight—to each factor based on how important it is to the outcome. If you're using a scale of 1 to 10, a weight of 10 means it's very important, while a weight of 1 means it's not very important.
4. **Rate the options.** Rate each option for each factor. Use a scale from 1 to 10, where 10 means the option is excellent in that factor and 1 means it's not good.
5. **Calculate weighted scores.** Multiply the rating by the weight for each factor.
6. **Add the scores.** Add up the scores for each option.
7. **Decide.** The option with the highest total score is usually the best choice, but you should also think about any other factors that might influence your decision.

centers or public libraries. Even local businesses might lend you a conference room.

Materials

Equip the room with plenty of square sticky notes about 3 inches (7.6 cm) or slightly larger. Choose ones big enough for legible writing but not so large that they quickly fill up wall space. Once wall space

Example: Choosing a Weekend Activity

Imagine you're trying to decide how to spend your weekend. You have three options: go to the movies, go bowling, or have a picnic. You decide that cost, fun, and time are the factors that matter to you.

1. **List the options:** movies, bowling, picnic
2. **Identify the criteria:** cost, fun, time
3. **Assign weights to criteria:**
   cost (weight 3), fun (weight 6), time (weight 1)
4. **Rate the options:**
   movies (cost 6, fun 8, time 5), bowling (cost 4, fun 9, time 7), picnic (cost 8, fun 7, time 4)
5. **Calculate weighted scores:**
   movies, (6×3) + (8×6) + (5×1) = 18 + 48 + 5
   bowling, (4×3) + (9×6) + (7×1) = 12 + 54 + 7
   picnic, (8×3) + (7×6) + (4×1) = 24 + 42 + 4
6. **Add the scores:**
   movies, 18 + 48 + 5 = 71
   bowling, 12 + 54 + 7 = 73
   picnic, 24 + 42 + 4 = 70
7. **Decide:** bowling is the best option, based on scores; other things to consider include who you'll be with, the weather, and any other factors that might influence the decision.

appears full, participants may subconsciously feel they've reached the end and stop thinking of new ideas.

Keep a supply of colored markers on hand. If you are using a whiteboard, be sure the markers are water-based. When using chart paper, stock up on fresh markers. But always test to ensure they don't bleed through the paper and stain walls or whiteboards. If you do have a mishap, acetone can often remove marker stains.

Case Study: Team Syphon

Remember Team Syphon from the Empathize chapter and their community partners Deyon and Jomari, who needed frequent airway clearing?

After learning more about the needs of Deyon and Jomari, the team started brainstorming ideas to prototype. How could they design something to improve the lives of their community partners? Jomari has cerebral palsy, which leaves him unable to move on his own. He depends on a tracheal tube inserted in his windpipe to ensure he gets enough air. This tube clogs up and must stay clear to maintain free breathing.

Deyon performs this life-sustaining responsibility when the tube clogs, about every three hours, day and night. This demanding schedule kept Deyon from getting enough sleep, which affected his health. His perpetual grogginess impaired his ability to concentrate and work. Lack of sleep was making Deyon's life miserable. Deyon needed a way to get his necessary sleep at night, while remaining confident Jomari would be safe and taken care of. After Team Syphon finished their empathy research and project definition, they were ready for ideation.

The members of Team Syphon generated many potential solutions to investigate in their ideation sessions. For example, one of their early ideas was to reduce the rate of mucus accumulation

Documenting Your Ideas

Documenting your ideation session is invaluable. Take photographs of sticky note arrangements before and after grouping. This practice helps if the original notes get lost or shuffled. Tools such as Google Lens or Microsoft Office Lens can convert these images into digital, editable text.

with a humidifying diffuser that would increase the moisture of the air around Jomari's tracheal tube. Manual suctioning would still be necessary but less frequent.

Team Syphon also sought feedback from members of other design teams at their school. As one team member said, "We would all come together [from our different teams] and talk about our projects . . . sometimes we were blind to the issues. They would come in with fresh eyes and point out, 'you could fix this and make it better.'" With further thought and this feedback, they pivoted to a more comprehensive solution. They went back to their empathy research and reexamined the need and the context.

They created an automated system that would turn on a suctioning machine when a sensor detected the tracheal tube needed clearing. Their sensor used room temperature, humidity, and the sound of Jomari's breathing to detect clogging and turn on a small motor for the suctioning machine.

Getting this constructive feedback turned out to be critical to Team Syphon's design project. In addition to helping Deyon and Jomari, the team wanted to create a design that might help other families in a similar situation. Their preliminary research showed that this was an ongoing issue for other people with tracheal tubes too. Hospitals and care facilities could also use this device. A simple, effective solution should be commercially successful.

Such documentation may prove vital since teams often revisit earlier ideas or even start fresh rounds of ideation. Going back to earlier design stages as needed is not a mistake. As Team Syphon showed, it's part of the iterative nature of design thinking. Once they had a deeper understanding of the situation, the team could redefine and refine their solution.

Tone

Set an upbeat, optimistic, and collaborative atmosphere. Ideally, participants should either have worked together well previously or show a genuine willingness to collaborate. Address any subgroup or individual conflicts before the ideation session. Conducting team-building exercises even before the Empathize phase can help in creating a harmonious environment, setting the stage for a successful design process.

All you really need for a successful ideation session is a comfortable, clean space that fosters collaboration. Even if the surroundings aren't perfect, the right group of people with a positive mindset can achieve exceptional results. As Margaret Mead famously said, "Never doubt that a small group of thoughtful, committed individuals can change the world. In fact, it's the only thing that ever has."

Before You Move On

In this chapter, we explored ideation, guiding you through its three key steps: brainstorming, affinity grouping, and selecting. Along the way, we shared proven techniques and tools to set your team up for success.

It's crucial to set the tone and assemble the right team in a productive workspace. It's equally important to strike a balance between seeking advice and trusting your team's process—a challenge that Team Syphon navigated skillfully when they showed their ability to adjust their project plan with feedback.

Effective brainstorming produces many excellent alternative solutions. Affinity clustering helps teams refine these ideas and identify the best choice for your community partners. Sometimes a fusion of multiple ideas emerges as the best option. For example, Team Squggle ingeniously merged three distinct needs into a singular, holistic solution for Chiara and Elena.

After concluding the Ideate phase, your team will have two or three promising concepts prepared for the Prototype phase. It's time to make and design things!

Ideate Checklist

- ⬡ Do you have two or three concepts you can prototype?
- ⬡ Do you have enough detail about each concept to build a prototype?

Reflection Questions

- Which of the three steps of ideation seems like the most fun?
- Which step might be the most work?
- Why not skip this phase entirely and just go with an obvious solution?
- Where would be a good location for you or your team to ideate?

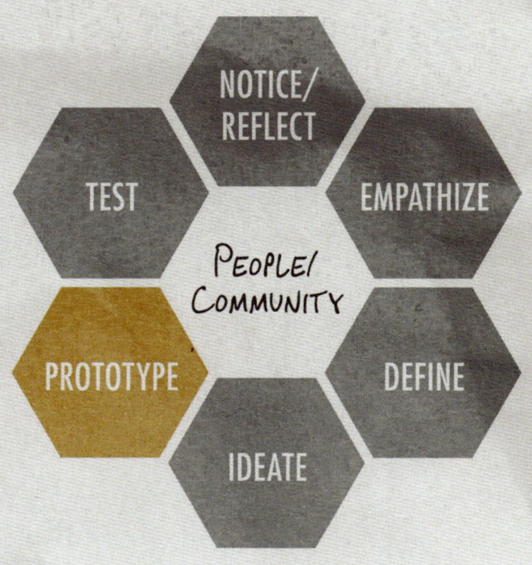

CHAPTER 5
Prototype

Occasionally, the designers made polished presentation models, but more often they were crude creations. Then, just as now, a prototype made out of foam core and a few rubber bands could be invaluable for sharpening an idea. One of the first prototypes of what would become the Apple mouse was just the ball from a roll-on deodorant stick and a butter dish from a Walgreens in Palo Alto [in California]. "All it had to do was illustrate a principle," [Jim Yurchenco, designer of the Apple mouse and holder of over eighty patents], says.

—2014 *WIRED* INTERVIEW WITH YURCHENCO

In prototyping, you quickly put together a working model—a rough draft—based on the solutions from the Ideate phase. Prototyping lets you visualize and test your concepts. Whether you're building devices or mapping processes, the goal isn't perfection but functionality.

The Prototype phase is a time to experiment, learn, and refine. Some designers call this "thinking by making." By engaging with these preliminary models, designers can gather invaluable feedback from community partners, ensuring the solution is on the right track.

Why Is Prototyping So Important?

Prototyping is a crucial step in design thinking because it brings abstract ideas to life. This essential phase allows for evaluation and refinement.

Prototyping makes it easy to visualize both the overall concept and its key components, spotlighting what works and what needs change. Early prototyping identifies potential issues, reducing the risk and cost of changes in later stages. This proactive approach helps ensure that minor glitches easily fixed during prototyping don't turn into significant flops for the community partner later on.

Prototypes offer a valuable opportunity for community partners to provide crucial feedback. Does this design address your problem? Does it make sense for your situation?

Prototyping fosters a mindset of "thinking by doing." Designers rough out their concepts early and often, avoiding the paralysis of perfectionism.

Prototyping helps to provide a quick yet critical examination of the design's feasibility, usability, and adaptability, ensuring the final product is well aligned with the community partner's needs and goals.

You Are Here in the Design Thinking Process

You and your design team have completed the Ideate phase and have several promising concepts. During the Prototype phase, you build these ideas in physical or visual models. Following the improvements during the Prototype phase, you will test these potential solutions.

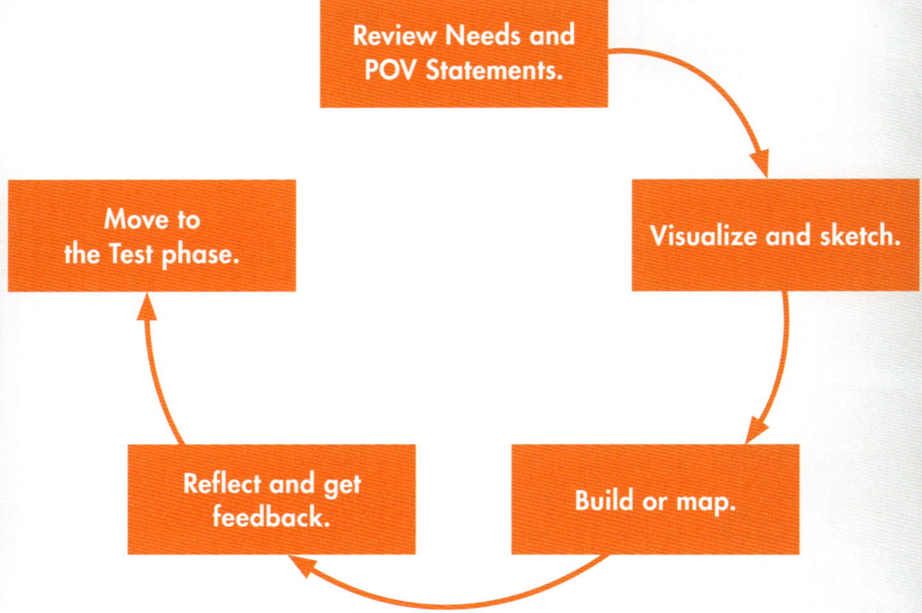

In this chapter, we'll bring ideas to life. You'll acquire the techniques of turning concepts into tangible forms, providing prototypes for testing and refining potential solutions. Specifically, you'll learn the following:

- Prototyping workflow, from visualizing and sketching to building and refining
- Types of prototypes—devices, processes, and digital creations
- Workspace requirements for prototyping
- Materials and tools that will be necessary for building prototypes
- The difference between low-resolution and high-resolution prototypes

Troubleshooting Prototype Challenges

Here are some common challenges and mistakes encountered during the Prototype phase, along with brief descriptions and suggestions on how to avoid them:

Overcomplicating the Prototype

CHALLENGE

Designers sometimes create a prototype that's too complex, trying to include every feature and detail.

SOLUTION

Start prototyping early. Even simple sketches or cardboard models can validate (or eliminate) an idea before you spend much effort. Focus these low-resolution prototypes on core features. The idea is to test concepts, not produce a finished product.

Falling in Love with Your First Idea

CHALLENGE

Designers sometimes become too attached to their first prototype, making them resistant to feedback.

SOLUTION

Cultivate an open mindset. Design thinking is iterative, and your first idea is rarely the best one.

Not Seeking Feedback from Community Partners

CHALLENGE

Some design teams get feedback exclusively from other team members and not from their community partners.

SOLUTION

Always check prototypes with your community partners to get genuine feedback. They'll interact with your prototype in unexpected ways, providing invaluable insights. View feedback as a gift, not a put-down. It's an opportunity to refine and improve your solution.

Making Your Prototype a Work of Art

CHALLENGE

Trying to make the prototype look visually appealing takes too much time away from improving the functionality of the prototype.

SOLUTION

Prioritize function in the initial stages of prototyping. Add visual appeal later.

Not Iterating Enough

CHALLENGE

After receiving feedback, some designers rush into finalizing a design without making several revisions.

SOLUTION

Don't rush the process. When collecting feedback, ask clarifying questions. Often, it's the repeated cycle of prototyping, testing, and iterating that leads to the best solutions.

Overlooking Limitations

CHALLENGE

Designers may forget about real-world limits such as budget, materials, or production.

SOLUTION

Always keep these natural boundaries in mind. If your prototype is too difficult to make, then it may not be a workable design. If in doubt, ask other experienced builders and makers for advice. Sometimes, a simple design change can make a tremendous difference.

These pitfalls underscore the importance of maintaining a flexible approach centered on your community partners throughout the Prototype phase. By knowing these common mistakes, designers can navigate the process more effectively and produce better prototypes.

Steps in Prototype Phase

Prototyping is a series of interconnected steps that guide designers from initial ideation to a tangible representation of a solution, whether physical, digital, or procedural. This flexible, iterative process ensures continual refinement based on feedback.

While outlining the prototyping stages that follow, note that every stage is crucial. Use your project journal to log your experiences at each step: challenges, breakthroughs, and observations. Regularly updating this journal ensures smooth transitions and captures all insights.

1. **REVIEW THE NEEDS AND POV STATEMENTS**
   Revisit your Needs and POV Statements. Use them as a reference to align your prototyping with your community partner's requirements. Identify the primary elements to highlight in your prototype.
2. **VISUALIZE AND SKETCH**
   Many designers begin with sketching rough ideas on paper, much as Leonardo da Vinci did in his notebooks. These initial sketches help crystallize ideas, providing a basic road map. Don't worry about your drawing ability—just get the idea down. These aren't artistic masterpieces. They are rough drafts of concepts.

   Think of a sketch as a two-dimensional prototype. Make multiple sketches from different views or blowups of certain parts. A time series or cartoon panel allows you to visualize designing a process. These sketches help the designer quickly explore a concept in several ways and get important initial feedback from other designers and community partners.

   Alternatively, some designers prefer diving into materials immediately, applying a "build to think" approach. They use low-resolution materials such as cardboard, pipe cleaners, foam, clay, and straws so they can work rapidly and make changes quickly.

When prototyping a process, consider borrowing the concept of an improvisational sketch from the performing arts. In design thinking, this is a brief acted-out scene to explore a case situation. Set the stage with a simple description, such as enhancing the client experience at a community clinic or training volunteers for a peer counseling program. Try out different approaches to the scene and pose potential issues as an experiment. Simple props and costumes are optional but make it more real—and more fun.

3. **BUILD OR MAP**

   Use your "sketches" to develop the next stage of your prototyping of devices, processes, or digital creations.

Prototyping Devices

Begin three-dimensional prototyping devices by crafting them from cheap, easy-to-shape, and easy-to-change materials. Many crafting materials are great for this stage of prototyping. With these low-resolution prototypes, you can see what your idea looks like in three dimensions and make multiple versions rapidly.

You can also prototype more than one idea. In addition, consider making a prototype of just one part of the device to focus on a critical feature, such as the shape or mechanism of a switch.

As the design progresses, you can make prototypes with higher resolution materials, such as hardwood, metal, and PVC, to make it sturdier and more permanent. A 3D printer can be a great prototyping tool if you have access to one.

Physical prototypes can have different stages as well. A first stage might be just a look-and-feel prototype. It doesn't work, but it gives the idea of what the end product could look like.

Case Study: Team Alertra

Prototyping captures the essence of design thinking as imaginative ideas meet real-world limitations. As Team Alertra worked on their wearable alarm device, they discovered the utility of creating prototypes.

The team had settled on making a wearable device to alert people with hearing impairment about dangers in the night, such as a fire. Batteries are the most common power source for wearable devices because they are lightweight and can store a lot of energy in a relatively small container.

The team could, in theory, design a sleek, comfortable case with a battery that fits perfectly. As they began prototyping, they quickly realized that wearable devices require several trade-offs, such as the size of the battery and the comfort of the device, along with its usability in daily living.

A bigger battery would have a longer life, fulfill power requirements, and require changing less often. Dev, handling the electronics, and Mark, creating the design of the casing, went back and forth several times making performance and wearability trade-offs.

Dev recalled wanting to start with the best electronic components available. Like most of us, he initially had no idea how many types of batteries there were and what they cost. Shortly after beginning to slog through a seemingly endless number of web pages, he focused on three criteria. The battery needed to meet the power requirements of their device, be readily available online, and fit within their budget. He soon navigated these trade-offs, and the team moved on.

Prototyping is not a straight-line trip but a journey along a winding road. It underscores the need for flexibility, adaptability, and a commitment to designing for and with your community partners.

Building prototypes brings your ideas to life.

Jeff Hawkins, a pioneer in handheld computers, wanted to find out how big he could make his PalmPilot. He prototyped this by cutting out blocks of wood in different sizes and carrying them around in his pockets. He also stuck sticky notes to some and practiced taking out his prototype and making notes with a golf pencil to simulate using a personal digital assistant. This combined both device prototyping and process prototyping.

Following a prototype that simply represents the size, shape, and major parts, a designer might build a functional model that can do some or all of what the product is supposed to do. You can add these working features in stages as you improve your prototypes.

At times, the prototype versions flow into one another, especially in electronics when using such tools as Arduino or micro:bits. With software and electronics, it is easy to get something up and working quickly. These tools are so good that the last prototype may sometimes be the first version of the actual product.

Prototyping Processes

Storyboards are a series of pictures or graphics showing how a process unfolds or how people might use a device. Paper and pencil are all you need to get started quickly with a storyboard. Free, easy-to-use storyboard software is available.

Skits and role-playing can also simulate processes, as discussed above. These skits are simple to do, and their versatility allows the team to switch time, place, and action rapidly. You can also videotape a skit and critique it later.

For example, IDEO used both physical models and role-playing to improve the experiences of patients at Kaiser Permanente. They built mock-ups of waiting rooms and exam rooms using sheets as walls and boxes as furniture. This allowed them to prototype different physical features of these spaces. Then they asked people to role-play patients with real staff and clinicians enacting typical scenarios. Since they could try out many "scripts," including unusual or high-risk situations, everyone learned a great deal. Later, they moved to actual rooms with proper equipment to try out specific scenarios in more depth.

Digital Prototyping

Designing digital products often means hybrid prototyping, since the project requires giving a set of instructions to a device or automating some process. For example, Team Syphon coded a sensor with instructions about the conditions that would notify Deyon that Jomari's tube needed attention. Team Alertra also coded a sensor to set off an alarm in case of a fire at night.

Prototyping software can be relatively easy, especially when you focus on the interface and key features without working out the full functionality. Successive prototypes might include more and more of the complete functions. A simple method, known as paper prototyping, involves one person acting as the community partner and another person simulating the response of the application to their partner's actions using paper and pencil. This method quickly spotlights design mistakes or potential flaws.

Tools such as MIT App Inventor offer easy-to-learn ways to get a fast start on developing app prototypes, especially for those new to software design. Twelve-year-old Gitanjali Rao, moved to action by the toxic pollution of water in Flint, Michigan, used App Inventor to develop the smartphone component of her invention to improve testing water for dangerous chemicals.

Many new app-based businesses start with a minimal viable product, which is a basic version of a product designed to gauge user interest and gather feedback. The designers then iteratively improve these minimal viable products based on customer input. Airbnb, Dropbox, and Reddit were all developed this way by digital entrepreneurs in their early to mid-twenties.

More and more businesses will involve combining hardware and software to improve some essential process in the lives of people. At the age of fifteen, Gitanjali created a device to detect opioids in blood within minutes. Gitanjali, an advocate of design thinking, developed her device, Epione, to help reduce the number of opioid-related deaths by making it easier to identify people who are at risk of addiction. Epione combines a microelectronic device with AI software, enabling this type of diagnostic process to move from a hospital with large, expensive equipment to a doctor's office. This project is an exciting glimpse of the future.

Prototyping Workspace

You can do prototyping in almost any versatile workspace, such as a garage or project room. Many communities have design labs or makerspaces available. A big, sturdy table with room for everyone to work is an excellent start. Find a room big enough for everyone to collaborate and move around comfortably. Stock it with easily adjustable materials for early prototyping stages, and have your ideation tools

accessible. Usually, the space you used for the Ideate phase will often work well if there are places for materials and tools.

It's vital to have space to store your prototypes, at least for the duration of the design project, so make sure there is ample storage. It's surprising how much room prototypes in progress occupy.

Will you need storage constraints for extended periods? Consider making your prototyping setup portable by organizing tools and materials in bins on a cart. Often, you can find an unused space to store the design cart and some prototypes. Even without a dedicated room, you can improvise a makeshift prototyping facility. With a flexible mindset, prototyping is possible virtually anywhere.

Materials and Tools

Prototyping is an invitation to work with many types of art and craft materials to bring your ideas to life. Start with easy-to-use materials, progressing to more durable ones as the design develops. In the Prototype phase, you're aiming to present your potential solutions in a way that makes sense for your community partner.

These materials and tools turn an idea into a physical or functional reality that the community partner can look at, play with, react to, and give feedback about. Try more than one way to prototype an idea to get multiple perspectives.

Materials

Low-resolution materials for the early stages of prototyping include duct tape, glue guns, foam core, cardboard, yarn, cloth, craft sticks, balsa wood (the lightweight wood used in model gliders), clay, and other easy-to-use, easy-to-change items.

Don't forget to keep your ideation bin at hand and stocked with sticky notes, markers, dry erase markers, pens and pencils, clear adhesive tape, dot stickers, and a flash drive.

A sudden inspiration sparked by a model might lead to further ideation. Often, you can do so much with these low-resolution materials that you can modify your prototypes enough to flow right into the Test phase with community partners.

Once your ideas are more fully developed, you can use more durable materials, such as wood, sheet metal, hard plastic, and PVC pipe to make your prototypes sturdier and give them more permanence. While these high-resolution materials require a bit more time to work with, the payoff can be well worth it for certain projects.

Tools

The only tools you need for low-resolution materials are utility scissors, a putty knife, a plastic cardboard cutter, or a utility knife. High-resolution materials often require shop tools for construction.

Low-Resolution Materials

Here is a starter list of easy-to-use, easy-to-change prototyping materials:

- cardboard
- clay
- duct tape
- foam core
- hot glue
- markers
- paper
- scissors
- tape
- bendable wire
- twist ties
- balsa wood
- craft sticks, such as those used for Popsicles and other frozen treats
- fabric scraps
- aluminum foil
- paper plates and cups
- pebbles made of stone or glass, such as those used in flower arranging
- soft modeling compound, similar to Play-Doh
- pipe cleaners
- rubber bands
- straws
- used-up whiteboard markers
- Lego bricks or other interlocking plastic blocks

These materials are all fairly inexpensive and easy to find, making them ideal for low-resolution prototyping. They are also easy to work with, even if you don't have a lot of experience with DIY projects.

Here are some tips for using low-resolution prototyping materials:

- **Don't worry about making your prototype look perfect.** The goal of low-resolution prototyping is to test your ideas quickly and cheaply, not to create a finished product.
- **Use materials that are easy to work with.** This will help you create your prototype quickly and easily.
- **Be creative and don't be afraid to experiment.** There are no rules for low-resolution prototyping materials. Use whatever you have on hand, and try to find the most creative and effective way to prototype your ideas. Your only limits are limitless boundaries of your imagination!

Exploring Innovative Prototyping Tools

Smartphones are a versatile prototyping tool. Use the camera to capture a photo story or create a video of a process. Try making an app with an app builder, or publish a simple, rough-draft website to test an idea for a community service. These digital platforms can be a great way to gather feedback from your community partners.

You can use a projector or a larger screen or smart TV to share ideas, especially if you've used your smartphone to create videos or photo stories. These visual aids allow for more interaction when presenting ideas to larger groups and asking for collaborative feedback.

If you're exploring electronic solutions, both micro:bits and Arduino are valuable assets. While micro:bits is more user-friendly, Arduino offers more versatility for more complex tasks. Teamed with a laptop, these microelectronics kits make it easy to test electronic ideas quickly.

For those with access to virtual reality (VR) or augmented reality (AR), these tools can offer immersive experiences, proving useful for prototyping. For example, AR and VR could raise environmental awareness. You might develop a VR experience depicting the effects of climate change on various ecosystems or an AR app showcasing endangered species in their natural habitats. A recent article in *Wired* magazine noted that the Save the Whales movement began when a naturalist released a tape of whale songs.

The tools for prototyping are always evolving, and new materials are continually emerging. Smart textiles with embedded sensors can interact with the environment, conductive ink allows for drawing electronic circuits on paper, and biodegradable materials offer environmentally friendly options. Let your imagination run wild and explore the possibilities!

Reflect and Get Feedback

Once you create a prototype, think about how well it meets the Needs and POV Statements. Then seek feedback from team members and

community partners. That feedback, along with your own judgment, will guide the next steps. This iterative approach, blending prototyping and testing, continually improves your design solution.

Feedback during prototyping is quick and informal, often done in simulated conditions in your workspace. Let team members or community partners interact with the prototype and make comments.

For example, Team Stria worked closely with Javier, their community partner, on a smart belt to avoid veering. They tried out multiple ideas and prototypes frequently, walking around the workspace and then on nearby sidewalks. This close collaboration produced a much better device, much more quickly.

Iterate or Move to Test Phase

This stage is a decision point in your prototyping workflow. Several possibilities are here, each implying a different path in your prototyping cycle, as the diagram shows.

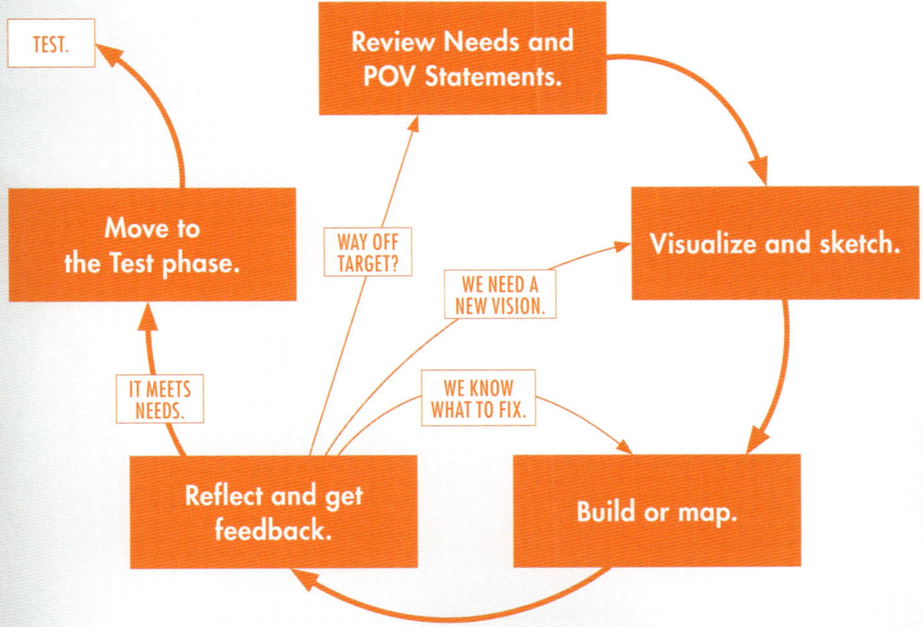

Case Study: William Kamkwamba's Windmill

Background

William Kamkwamba loved science, technology, and learning how machines worked. "Before I discovered the wonders of science, I was just a simple farmer in a country of poor farmers," he said in his 2009 TED talk. William and his community in Malawi, a nation in East Africa, faced immense adversity when a severe famine struck their village.

Forced to drop out of school, William's insatiable curiosity led him to read daily in a local library. There, he discovered the book *Using Energy*, which included a chapter on generating electricity from the wind. He realized a windmill could pump water from the family well to water the parched crops. This discovery sparked his visionary quest to build a windmill to generate electricity for his family and the community.

Prototyping

William realized that he could experiment with his windmill design by building a small model before attempting a full-scale version. Guided by this insight and pictures from *Using Energy*, he constructed a prototype using materials scavenged from around his house and the village dump. These included PVC pipe, bicycle spokes, and an electric motor repurposed from his father's old cassette music player.

With the help of a friend, he hooked up his prototype windmill to a small radio and raised it on a bamboo pole. As they watched, the wind blew, the blades turned, and the radio played. It worked! This was the proof he needed to build a windmill big enough for the village. He whooped, "Now I go even bigger. Superpower!"

Learnings and Iteration

Making and testing the prototype windmill were crucial for William's project. He grasped the mechanics of harnessing wind energy, spotted

One of William's first windmills bringing electricity to his village in Malawi

design flaws, and made necessary adjustments. The insights gained from this stage played a crucial role in the construction of a larger, fully functional windmill.

Impact

William's ingenuity and perseverance resulted in the construction of a windmill that not only powered his family's home but also brought about significant improvements to the living conditions of his community. His story demonstrates the power of prototyping and its potential for turning vision into reality, even with few resources.

Did the feedback show that the design was sound but that this prototype needed some fixes that were easy or obvious? Then you and the team can simply go back to building and reworking.

Did the feedback suggest that the overall approach was right but that this prototype had some big flaws or was missing some important features? Then you and the team may need to return to the visualize and sketch stage to add to or change the existing design.

Possibly, the feedback revealed that this design solution was way off and did not provide a solution for the community partners. Then you and the team need to go back and carefully review the Needs and the POV Statements along with your community partners. What did you miss? What did you not understand? You and the team may need to rethink your entire approach before continuing back through the visualize and sketch stage and then the build or map stage.

Learn and continue through the cycle. Make it. Try it. Do it again better. You may go back to earlier stages one or many times. This quick prototyping cycle is a hallmark of design thinking. It is a key to why design thinkers can move rapidly to make better and more innovative solutions for community partners.

What if the feedback is overwhelmingly positive? As you and the team reflect on this prototype, does it align well with the Needs and POV Statements? Is it practical to build, and does it fit within your budget? Does it seem ready for the rigors of real-world trials? If so, then it's *almost* time to move to the Test phase. Yay!

Almost? Yes. First, document your reflections, learnings, and the rationale behind your decisions here. Briefly discuss the alignment with your community partner's Needs and POV Statements. Are there any small or lingering concerns about the practicality? These insights will help during testing and guide the design of your tests.

In the next chapter on the Test phase, we'll focus on carefully assessing these later prototypes to determine how well they fit the criteria of the Needs and POV Statements. After design teams receive

constructive assessments, they often go back to earlier stages of prototyping or even earlier phases of design, such as Empathize, Notice and Reflect, Define, or Ideate.

Before You Move On

In this chapter, we learned about the Prototype phase in design thinking following a five-step prototyping workflow model. Three key elements of prototyping are experimentation, feedback, and iteration. Perfection is not the goal. "Perfect enough" is a helpful motto.

Prototyping is a learning process. We take our ideas, build them, learn from the feedback, and get ready for real-world testing in the Test phase.

Prototype Checklist

- ○ Have you completed one or more prototypes ready for real-world testing in the Test phase?
- ○ Have you updated your design project journal with these summaries:
  - Major revisions to the prototype and rationale
  - Team learnings on challenges and solutions
  - Key feedback from community partners and others
  - Lists of materials and tools used
  - Photo documentation
- ○ Have you backed up any digital work?

Reflection Questions

- Where might you locate your workspace?
- Do you have a source for materials and tools?
- What part or parts of prototyping seem most challenging? Most fun?
- How might issues of equity play out in prototyping?

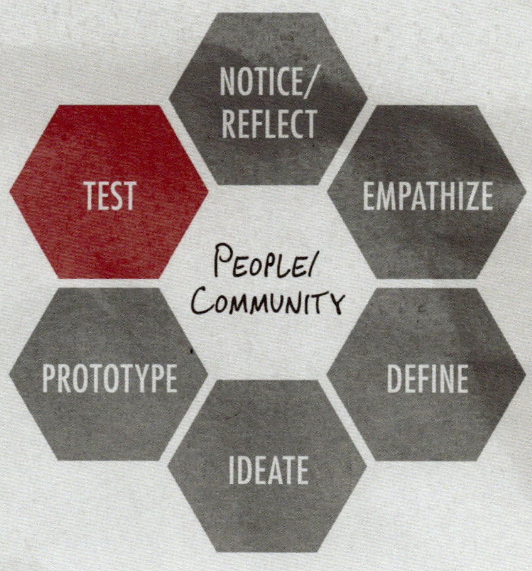

CHAPTER 6

Test

We went to [our community partners'] house to test our project, Squggle, but it just wasn't working. This was so very disappointing, and it really brought us down. But it also drove us to figure it out.

—LILLI OF TEAM SQUGGLE

In design thinking, testing is the final phase. The team presents the refined prototype to community partners and stakeholders for a thorough evaluation. This phase systematically pushes the prototype's capabilities, compares its performance against the Needs and POV Statements, and identifies areas for improvement.

While the Prototype phase involves quick, small-scale tests of rough designs for iterative improvements, the Test phase is more rigorous and comprehensive. It assesses a more polished design's effectiveness, usability, and impact to determine whether the solution addresses the identified problem.

Getting bad news early, like Team Squggle did, can be a gift and help you make your design better faster. This chapter covers the basics of testing and shows how testing connects to each of the other steps in the design process.

Why Is Testing So Important?

Testing allows designers to examine their prototypes in real-life conditions, uncovering essential insights for refinement. It verifies the solution's success in meeting community partners' needs. The designers resolve any potential issues before implementation. This thorough assessment not only reduces the risk of a flawed solution but also leads to more innovation and a deeper understanding of community partners.

You Are Here in the Design Thinking Process

You've made it to the Test phase, the last step of design thinking. As you test, you'll see if your prototype meets all the goals in the Needs and POV Statements. If not, no problem. Loop back to the Prototype phase or even an earlier stage, depending on what the feedback says.

Iterate through the design phases until your prototype satisfies your community partner. Once that's done, you and the team have crossed the finish line. Time for some well-earned celebration with your community partners!

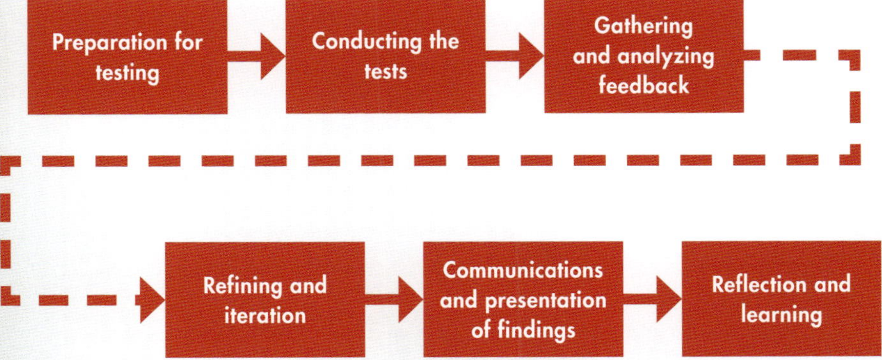

In this chapter, you'll discover how to test the prototypes you built, finding what works as well as what does not work *yet*. The iterative cycle of feedback from testing may take you back to fixing a prototype or even further, perhaps rethinking your basic concept or even reformulating your understanding of the need. Specifically, you'll learn

- How to plan for testing
- Who to include in the testing process
- How to run a prototype test
- How to use the test results to strategize your next steps

Troubleshooting the Test Phase

A variety of challenges can emerge during the Test phase in design thinking. These may include the following:

Emotional Attachment

CHALLENGE

Designers may become too attached to their prototypes, which can result in resistance to essential feedback.

SOLUTION

Remind your team that revision is a necessary part of the design process. Regularly revisit the project's original objectives and success criteria to maintain focus. Ensure that any change aligns with the project's Needs and POV Statements.

Overwhelmed from Excessive Feedback

CHALLENGE

Managing a large volume of feedback can be overwhelming, posing a challenge in sifting through comments and risking the loss of crucial insights.

SOLUTION

Prioritize the feedback starting with comments that are connected to the Needs and POV Statements and that have a substantial impact on the project. The techniques discussed in the Ideate phase, such as categorizing feedback into themes to identify patterns, can make data more manageable.

Chasing Perfection

CHALLENGE

A desire to respond to every piece of feedback can distract designers from the original objectives. It may also lead to the unnecessary expansion of project objectives based on feedback. This causes delays and uses more resources.

SOLUTION

Striking a balance is key. Focus on implementing changes that make a big difference and are in line with the project's objectives. Only make changes that will genuinely enhance the design. Not every piece of feedback will help or apply.

Ethical Considerations

CHALLENGE

The Test phase introduces various ethical considerations, such as respecting participant privacy and addressing any unintended consequences of the design.

SOLUTION

Upholding a high standard of ethics is essential throughout the Test phase. Ensure participant confidentiality, maintain transparency about data usage, and get informed consent. Regularly assess the potential impact of your design on the community and address any negative consequences. Integrating ethical considerations throughout design thinking is vital to developing solutions that are innovative, responsible, and respectful to all stakeholders involved.

Case Study: Team Squggle

Lilli and Avery wanted to help their community partners, Chiara, a nine-year-old girl, and Elena, her mom, with several problems. Chiara has cerebral palsy with quadriplegia. She is neither verbal—though she and her mom communicate with vocalizations—nor mobile, spending much of her time in bed. Chiara has some limited use of her hands.

Elena, when working in other parts of the house, wants to know that her daughter is OK and comfortable. She asked Lilli and Avery to address four challenges:

- Communication—a way for Chiara to signal when she needs her mom
- Stimulation—a gadget to entertain Chiara
- Comfort—a mechanism to help relax Chiara when she is feeling stressed
- Engagement—a toy to play with and ease her boredom and sense of isolation

Avery and Lilli learned in their empathy interviews that Chiara liked stuffed plushie toys. They envisioned a fun yet functional solution for both mother and daughter and brainstormed an idea for a plushie toy with an embedded communications device, which they called Squggle.

Squggle has a vibrating motor inside that turns on when squeezed, providing stimulation and engagement. These vibrations can also help soothe Chiara when she is tense. And squeezing Squggle also generates a signal to Elena's cell phone, giving Chiara the ability to communicate with her mom remotely so Elena could know when Chiara needed her.

Avery and Lilli prototyped Squggle in their workshop, ironing out sensor and circuit problems. Finally, Squggle was ready for testing with Chiara and Elena. Avery and Lilli were excited and looked forward to seeing Chiara with Squggle. But on the day of their first test, everything seemed to go wrong.

***Left to right*: Avery and Lilli demonstrate their Squggle invention.**

It was quickly obvious that the squeeze mechanism was too stiff. Chiara could not activate the sensor that started the vibrating motor and the Bluetooth communications to Elena's cell phone. And the internal mechanisms inside the toy came loose after a bit of play.

Lilli and Avery were disappointed. Elena pointed out that Chiara liked the look and feel of the plushie toy design, and she liked the basic concept of Squggle. Lilli and Avery realized they could improve the prototype. A field test can reveal necessary changes.

Following this test, they went back to their workshop to improve Squggle. They increased the sensitivity of the pressure sensor so Chiara could operate it easily and designed more secure fastenings for the internal mechanism so Chiara's Squggle could stand up to daily use. After a few more iterations, Squggle was a hit with Chiara and Elena. Reflecting later, Avery and Lilli knew that although the initial disappointment of testing was hard, the testing made Squggle a success.

Steps in Test Phase

After all the prototyping, it is time to test your design in the real world.

Preparation for Testing

1. **DEFINE SUCCESS CRITERIA**

   Start by clearly defining what success looks like for your prototype. What do you want to learn from this testing session? Are you testing a device, a process, or both? What do you want to know about the prototype? What are the big questions on the minds of the design team? This step, based on the Needs and POV Statements, sets the guidelines for evaluating results and refining the design.

2. **DEVELOP A TEST PLAN**

   Next, create a detailed and organized test plan that orders the testing steps. Outline what elements of the prototype you will test, identify the participants, and describe the testing methods. Find and arrange the materials and space needed for testing.

   It may be possible to test two or more prototypes in one test session. Sometimes you will need to focus only on how well one very critical part of a device works, such as the sensor for Jomari's breathing tube. Or you can focus on one part of a community partner's experience with your service or process, such as how swimmers in the Scandinavian town got to and from the pool.

   Don't forget to specify what information to record and how to record it. Do you need a formatted data sheet? A pad of paper and clipboard work well for capturing your data, as does a laptop. Voice notes on a phone can work, though you won't be able to see the data emerge in real time and won't get the data in a particular format.

A team of Australian students at the University of Technology Sydney test their prototype of a Smart Bin. The bin separates recyclables automatically.

3. **SELECT PARTICIPANTS**

Recruit your community partners as testers. This is simple if your community partners are already a part of the design team. Or get others involved to offer fresh perspectives, as the community partners who have been designing with you are now insiders. If you are working with more than one testing participant at a time, the focus group information in the Empathize chapter may be helpful.

Include a diverse range of participants to gain a variety of viewpoints and insights. Lilli and Avery, for example, originally designed Squggle specifically for Chiara, so her responses were the most important. But if Lilli and Avery think Squggle might help more people besides Chiara and Elena, then they would plan for broader testing. A more inclusive selection leads to richer feedback and a design solution that is more likely to meet the diverse needs of the community.

4. **CREATE A COMFORTABLE ENVIRONMENT**
   Create a testing environment where participants feel comfortable. Ensuring that participants feel valued and heard encourages more authentic responses and more insightful feedback. You do not want participants holding back critical comments out of misplaced politeness or to avoid confrontation. For many tests, your designing workspace may work perfectly, as long as there is enough privacy for candor.

   Sometimes, you need to test the prototypes in real-world conditions, perhaps in a specific location, with special equipment, or with particular participants. For such field testing, make sure that all necessary materials and equipment are available and ready to go. Make these tests as close to everyday reality as possible.

   For example, after initial indoor testing of their smart band that helps blind people avoid veering, Team Stria and their community partner Javier tested the device on streets near his home.

Conducting the Tests

This step is your chance to interact with community partners and gather invaluable feedback. Use these guidelines for a smooth and productive testing session:

1. **MANAGE EXPECTATIONS**
   Start by clearly setting and managing the expectations of community partners. Make sure they understand the development stage of the prototype and the type of feedback you are seeking.
2. **RUN YOUR TEST**
   One or more designers work with community partners during a trial run of the prototype for a product or process.

The partners describe how well the prototype is working and their thoughts about how it will work in actual use.

Learn and apply facilitation techniques to conduct testing sessions effectively. Ask open-ended questions and encourage honest feedback to gather valuable insights.

- How well does the prototype work?
- Is it easy to use? Is it durable enough?
- Is it convenient to use and store when not in use?
- Is it dangerous in some way?
- Is it fun to use?
- Is it elegant?

Think of Apple products as an inspiration for the later stages of usability testing.

3. **OBSERVE SKILLFULLY**

The designers listen, observe, and document the testing. They pay attention to what the test participants do and say, as well as their reactions. Capture both verbal and nonverbal reactions. Did someone's eyes light up with a certain feature? Is a device working as they expect? Do the testers learn how to operate the device or how to follow the process quickly? Is a process missing a step?

Facial expressions and body language convey a lot of information and are just as important as spoken feedback. Actively listen and take detailed notes to capture all aspects of the experience of test participants.

4. **INCORPORATE FEEDBACK**

Encourage candid and critical feedback during testing. Be prepared to receive both positive and negative feedback. Accept all comments gracefully, and use them as appropriate to improve the prototype. You do not want people to hold back on their feedback because they think it will offend you or cause you extra work or expense.

5. **ITERATE DURING TESTING**

Be flexible and open to making real-time adjustments to the prototype based on immediate feedback. Getting too attached to the current version keeps you from making a better one. Adaptability leads to more effective solutions and generates trust from your community partners.

Testing also reveals possibilities. "What if we merged these two ideas?" or "Oh, oh! We forgot about that essential function!" or "Wow, we need something entirely different!" All of these are important discoveries.

Gathering and Analyzing Feedback

Uncover the insights from your prototype's performance with the analysis.

1. **DOCUMENT THE TEST**

Capture the reactions of the testing participants and your discussions with them as they interact with the prototype. Smartphone photos, video, and audio recording catch important expressions, movements, and body language. Have measuring tools, such as stopwatches or tapes, for numerical data. Have paper and pencils on hand for quick sketches or noting ideas.

One designer can work with the participant and facilitate the test, while another designer handles the recording.

After the test, you can transcribe any audio or video recordings, if needed. Transcribing by hand gives extra insight about the actual interaction but takes a long time. Many smartphone apps and digital platforms have built-in audio-to-text transcription that can be generated in real time, saving your team valuable effort.

2. **ANALYZE DATA AND REFLECT ON FEEDBACK**

Once you have your data, look for patterns, connections, and outliers in the feedback. Combine the numbers and the narratives. Numerical data, such as ratings or times, give you measurable aspects of your prototype's performance, forming a frame for evaluation.

Qualitative data, on the other hand, provides the stories and experiences behind those numbers. It fills in the picture and should get the most weight in your evaluation. Together, numerical and qualitative data offer a well-rounded perspective on where your prototype stands.

Make notes about improvements in the prototype, as well as improvements in their design and testing. Tacking photos from the test onto the design lab walls helps guide this analysis. What's working well? Where are the stumbling blocks?

Compare these findings with your initial objectives and success criteria. Pause and think about the feedback received. What implications does it have for the project? Don't be defensive about feedback. This is how you improve. Keep a growth mindset!

3. **PRIORITIZE CHANGES**

Not all feedback points carry the same weight. Some requests might be easy fixes, while others may require more thought and resources. Prioritize based on the impact on your community partners and the feasibility of making these adjustments.

Refining and Iteration

After gathering and analyzing all the valuable feedback, apply what you have learned.

1. **ADJUST THE DESIGN SOLUTION**
   Based on the feedback you've collected, start making the necessary modifications to your prototype. Every piece of feedback is a gift that helps you improve. Look at what worked and what didn't, and adjust your design accordingly.
2. **EVALUATE TRADE-OFFS**
   If you adjust the design solution, you may need to make some trade-offs. For example, Team Alertra, in creating an alarm wristband for people who are hard of hearing, decided to delay connecting their alarm wristband with 911 to get the band to people who need it sooner. Connecting with 911 is an excellent feature but would take a long time to finish. You always need to balance the needs of the community partners with good-to-have features, your budget, and your timelines.
3. **RETEST**
   After adjusting the design, you may want to retest your refined prototype, depending on the size and impact of the change. For significant changes, invite your community partners to review the improved prototype. The immediate design team may test minor fixes.
4. **DOCUMENT CHANGES**
   Keep notes on all the adjustments made and the insights gained during this phase in your design project journal. This documentation will help with the final evaluation.
5. **UPDATE OBJECTIVES**
   If your adjustments have led to significant changes in the prototype, you may need to revise your project's objectives and success criteria. Keep your overall goals clearly focused when iterating the Needs or POV Statements.
6. **REFINEMENT AND ITERATION**
   Improve your design in a cycle of learning. With each iteration, you're making your solution more effective.

Communication and Presentation of Findings

Once you've tested your prototype and gathered feedback, it's time to share your innovation. This is when you synthesize your insights, prepare a clear, compelling presentation, and strategize your next steps.

1. **PRESENT RESULTS**

   Communicate your findings with community partners or stakeholders clearly and simply. How will you engage your audience? Highlight the key findings, the changes made, and the reasons behind them in a logical flow. Be prepared to answer questions and explain your design choices. Your design project journal will help here.

   Different audiences may require different presentations. Your community partners will care most about how the features and functions achieve the objectives of the Needs and POV Statements. Potential funders will focus on scalability, costs, and alternative solutions in the market. As in the Oakland park and the Scandinavian pool examples, local governments will prefer to hear how this change will affect all members of the community, as well as municipal regulations or systems.

   Visualizing data can make a substantial difference. Use graphs, charts, or other visual aids such as simple infographics to make your findings more accessible and comprehensible. These aids help your audience grasp the complex ideas and the significance of your results.

2. **ASK FOR ADDITIONAL FEEDBACK**

   When presenting your findings, encourage an open dialogue. Invite your audience to ask questions, provide additional feedback, or even challenge your conclusions. This interactive approach not only enhances understanding but could provide further insights.

Navigating the Implementation Stage

This book focuses on the six core steps of design thinking. As you finish testing and your community partner likes and accepts your design solution, you may think about how to implement your solution in the real world. While this could be an entire book in itself, this section outlines some steps to get you started and offers additional implementation resources.

Decide on the Type of Implementation

Is your solution limited to your original community partners? Or might you consider wider distribution? For example, could this be a commercial product? Or might you give it to a foundation? Each will require a different plan.

Stay Engaged with Your Community Partners

Your community partners are crucial for the successful real-world application and adaptation of your solution. Ongoing communication and collaboration ensure a design solution that will meet their needs and expectations.

Plan Your Resources

Assess and strategically allocate the necessary resources—time, finances, and personnel—to continue implementing your solution. Develop a detailed and realistic budget and timeline, keeping in mind potential challenges and preparation for the unexpected. Plan ahead for a smooth implementation.

3. **PLAN NEXT STEPS**

   As your presentation wraps up, outline the next steps. Depending on the feedback, this could mean further prototyping and refinement, preparing for the implementation, or even going back to the ideation drawing

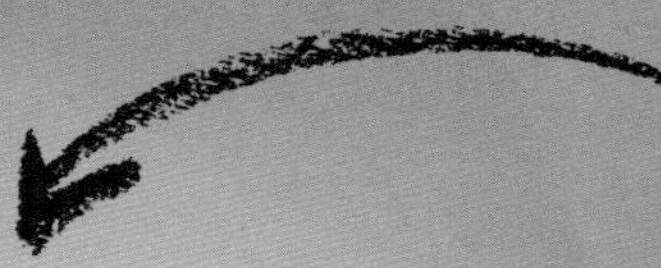

Monitor and Evaluate Your Plan

Define clear measures of the success criteria early in the implementation process. Regularly monitor the progress and evaluate the impact of your solution, adjusting strategies based on feedback and your observations.

Assess Scalability and Sustainability

Consider the longer-term future of your project. Can it grow naturally and sustainably? What ongoing support will you need? How might it develop to create a lasting impact?

Document and Share Your Knowledge

Thoroughly document each step of the implementation process, noting challenges encountered and lessons learned. Your insights and discoveries can help you and your team as the implementation progresses. Your records also help those who come later and may not have taken part in the initial development project.

Learn Continually

Approach the implementation stage with a mindset of continual learning and improvement. Stay receptive to improving your solution as you gain more insights, both from your own real-world application experience and from the wisdom of others.

For a deeper exploration of implementation strategies, consider exploring reputable sources such as specialized books, scholarly articles, online courses, and professional organizations focusing on project management and design thinking implementation. I list some of these in the Going Further section.

board to explore new solutions. This step of the Test phase continues the design conversation and supports the collaborative approach to problem-solving you have cultivated. Meaningful collaboration translates your team's design into real-world implementation.

Case Study: Stinky the Robot

Although it sounds like a Hollywood fantasy, the true story of four students, Lorenzo Santillan, Luis Aranda, Oscar Vasquez, and Cristian Arcega, along with their teachers Fredi Lajvardi and Allan Cameron, showcased remarkable problem-solving skills, resourcefulness, and teamwork. Their experience exemplifies the interplay between prototyping and testing and how iterative refinement can lead to success.

In 2004 this team of four immigrant teenagers from Carl Hayden Community High School in Arizona faced off against several universities, including MIT, in the Marine Advanced Technology Education Remotely Operated Vehicle Competition. With limited resources, they exhibited an extraordinary level of ingenuity, resourcefulness, and determination to build their robot, affectionately named Stinky. Though this was the first robot any of them had ever built, they would need to design it to complete several tricky challenges, such as extracting a liquid sample from a sunken barrel.

By necessity, the team used affordable, everyday materials to build Stinky, such as a waterproof briefcase found on sale at a local store to use as the outer shell. Many of the competing college teams used expensive composite materials or machined aluminum, things that the Carl Hayden students could only dream about.

But these limitations forced them to improvise and innovate. For example, the hollow PVC pipe frame they used was very buoyant, so Stinky would need added weight to stay underwater and complete the contest challenges. Cristian suggested putting the heavy car battery that would power Stinky on the PVC frame to hold it down. This added the needed weight, but one small leak would destroy the electrical wiring and end their hopes.

As they discussed this idea, someone pointed out that the other teams would probably keep their battery on the deck of the pool. "If we do the same thing as everyone else, we'll finish last," Cristian said, "because they've done it before." They tested the decision to put the battery on the frame, along with their other innovations, at a local dive store, since their school had no pool.

Lorenzo's solution for extracting liquid from the barrel also required many prototype-test-fix cycles. Some of their competitors used electronically controlled three-way valves, multiple pumps, and syringes for measuring the exact amount of liquid the contest required. Lorenzo rigged copper tubing to a basement sump pump and attached a balloon to hold the liquid. With a lot of testing, he found he could get just the right amount of liquid by figuring out the pump's flow rate with a stopwatch.

But the heavy balloon kept slipping off the end of the copper pipe. He tried several ways to keep the balloon in place to deliver the liquid to a testing station. None worked. Then he had the idea to use a liter soda bottle rescued from the recycling bin to hold the balloon in place. That worked—after many more trials.

Their iterative process of prototyping, testing, and refinement paid off. The Carl Hayden High School team's innovative design and problem-solving abilities led them to a surprising and inspiring victory against well-resourced college teams, highlighting the power of determination and an iterative design thinking approach. The team's story became a Hollywood film, as well as the award-winning book *Spare Parts: Four Undocumented Teenagers, One Ugly Robot, and the Battle for the American Dream* by Joshua Davis.

When You Haven't Achieved Your Goals . . . *Yet*

Is it possible to run out of time or money before you and the team have achieved the project objectives and delighted your community partner? Yes! In the real world, projects may take longer or cost more than expected, or priorities may shift for your team or community partner.

Even so, you, your team, and your community partners have learned more about the problem, potential solutions, design thinking, and yourselves. And frank discussion and creative thinking in collaboration with your community partners can usually lead to alternative solutions that still make a positive change. As Supreme Court justice Oliver Wendell Holmes said, "A mind once stretched by a new experience can never go back to its old dimensions."

Think about the challenges facing the underwater robotics team. Their underfunded public school had few resources to support the robotics team, money was tight for all their families, none of them had ever built a robot before, and the immigration authorities might pick up and deport three of the four with no warning. And the competition these high school students entered was highly competitive with many well-resourced college teams. Yet they prevailed through hard work and perseverance.

Embrace a growth mindset, check all your assumptions, and test all the limits. Nelson Mandela said, "It always seems impossible until it is done." Additional resources often materialize when a team is passionate and determined. The robotics team impressed many people with their positive attitude and hard work. Some of these people stepped in at critical points to support the team, sometimes with a little cash, sometimes with the loan of a piece of equipment they could not buy, or sometimes with some expert advice on robotics.

And the team's inspirational teachers coached, encouraged, supported, and believed in them all along the way. In Apple Computer's "Think Different" campaign, Steve Jobs said, "The people who are crazy enough to think they can change the world are the ones who do."

Reflection and Learning

At the close of the Test phase, pause and reflect. Reflection isn't just looking back but also learning and planning for the future.

Investigate what went well and what confused or derailed you during the Test phase. What have you learned from your community partners' feedback and your observations? Were there any surprises that caught you off guard? How inclusive was your approach? Did you involve all segments of the community? How well did you work as a team? What else might help your team improve?

Reflection guides the entire design thinking process, while integrating your experience builds confidence.

Before You Move On

The goal of the Test phase is to get information about how well the prototype works. Is the prototype ready to launch into the real world? What worked? What didn't work? What could be better? Frequently, following testing, the team will go back to the Prototype phase, or even back to the drawing board. This may lead the designers back to check their empathy research, refine their definition, rethink their prototype, change their idea, or generate a whole new concept.

These are not failures but commitments to growth and quality. Each step during testing is to help gain greater insights into the problem, the needs of the people, and the context of the problematic situation. You return to and iterate until you satisfy the requirements of the Needs and POV Statements.

This stage is so necessary and can also be fun. It puts you in closer touch with your community partners, and you learn much more about your own process or product.

As you can see from the Design Thinking for Innovation and Social Impact model, the Test phase is the last phase in design thinking. But since design thinking is highly iterative, you and your team will no doubt move back and forth between the six phases.

Test Checklist

- ⬡ Have you carried out enough tests with a diverse set of participants to gather a wide range of feedback?
- ⬡ Have you systematically analyzed feedback for areas of improvement from all test participants?
- ⬡ Have you iterated and refined your prototype based on the feedback received? Then retested?
- ⬡ Have you evaluated the final design against the original objectives and success criteria?
- ⬡ Have you reviewed and addressed all ethical considerations?
- ⬡ Have you communicated and shared the key findings with your community partners and stakeholders?
- ⬡ Have you reflected on what you learned during this phase and how it can be applied in future projects?
- ⬡ Have you celebrated your successes and the progress made with your team and community partners?

Reflection Questions

- What challenges did you encounter during the Test phase, and how did you overcome them? Would you approach these challenges differently in the future?
- How did you prioritize and implement the feedback received?
- Did you experience any emotional attachment to your initial design? How did this impact your receptiveness to feedback and willingness to make changes?
- How did you handle ethical considerations during the Test phase? Were there any unforeseen ethical dilemmas, and how were they resolved?
- Based on your experiences in this phase, how might you approach testing differently in future projects?

CONCLUSION

Remember the design team who developed a smart belt to help blind people avoid drifting into hazards such as traffic? There's more to this story. Entering their Stria smart band in several invention competitions, the team won the AT&T Inventor's Challenge and the SXSW EDU Student Impact Challenge, along with over $3,000 in prize money.

Team member Nolyn described the team as "almost like a small start-up. We're able to share ideas and grow as designers and as people, creating a quality product for users who are blind." Encouraged, they took the leap to bring their invention to the aid of more people like Javier.

Incorporating as a business called Stria Labs, the team is filing for a patent on the Stria band. They continue to collaborate with centers for the blind community across the country and to interview visually impaired people as part of their continual development.

Nolyn said, "Personally, I've learned a lot about interacting with people like teammates, helping toward a common goal. But also, I've learned about the struggles that people in our community face every single day that we might not be aware of."

The Stria Labs team will start premarket launch testing soon, making the final improvements needed to bring the Stria band to more people as a commercial product. Stria Labs is also developing an app to use cloud technology to offer improved guidance for walking. Besides alerting people about veering, the team plans to integrate enhanced navigation into the Stria band to help people walk from their starting point to their destination.

The Stria band has come so far from its beginnings as a high school invention project toward its goal of bringing a better, safer life to visually impaired people. As team member Maya said, "I've always wanted to do something big to help the world. It's hard to really make a difference in a few months, but Javier won't be veering into traffic anymore."

Innovations often begin in university labs and then become start-up companies. Stria Labs is at the forefront of a promising trend in innovation where high school design labs incubate start-up companies. Naturally, not every design thinking project by students makes it this far, just as many inventions by experienced engineers and product designers with venture capital backing don't always succeed. The Stria team and the other teams in this book are in the lead.

Key Ideas

This book presents an easy-to-follow approach to design thinking and aims to empower changemakers and provide essential information for tackling community issues. Each chapter explains one phase of the process model with step-by-step instructions. The stories of real student teams provide practical guidance for designing solutions that promote social good.

In this concluding chapter, let's bring the concepts full circle by recapping the essence of design thinking and its powerful impact on communities when applied with thoughtfulness and creativity. Three important themes run through this guide:

1. **THE IMPORTANCE OF COLLABORATION AND TEAMWORK**
2. **THE NECESSITY OF CONTINUAL REFLECTION AND ADAPTATION BASED ON FEEDBACK**
3. **THE CYCLICAL NATURE OF DESIGN THINKING, WHICH MAY TAKE THE TEAM BACK THROUGH EARLIER PHASES SEVERAL TIMES, BASED ON REFLECTION AND FEEDBACK**

Notice and Reflect

Begin a project by noticing and reflecting about your community partners. As a team, consider your roles, reasons, and responsibilities in this situation. Be mindful of your own thoughts, emotions, and biases in this context. Investigate the entire ecosystem of the problem before rushing to brainstorm solutions.

Empathize

Develop a deep personal understanding of the challenges and realities faced by the community partners you are designing with. Engage in conversation with your community partners, observing and listening to them. Ensure that your thought process is genuinely centered on addressing the needs of others and not just based on your own preconceptions of what your community partners require.

As you navigate through design thinking, pause and periodically reflect on the impact of your actions and assumptions. Question yourself: Are the changes I'm making building a more equitable and inclusive community?

Define

When formulating problem statements, focus on the needs of individuals rather than on devices or new processes. Repeatedly ask "Why?" until you uncover the most fundamental need of your community partner, ensuring that you address the root cause rather than a superficial issue.

Ideate

During the brainstorming phase, aim to generate as many ideas as possible. Suspend judgment, as seemingly outlandish ideas can often pave the way for groundbreaking solutions.

Prototype

Create simple prototypes of your concepts quickly using accessible materials, as well as making drawings and diagrams. Thinking with your hands may reveal new insights.

Test

Try out your prototypes early and often with your community partners. Realize that failing early on, coupled with continual refinement, achieves better solutions more quickly than plodding perfectionism.

Remember to

- **Collaborate** with team members and your community partners to understand the problem and gather diverse perspectives (Notice and Reflect, Empathize, and Define phases).
- **Reflect** on the insights gathered, prototypes developed, and feedback received (Ideate and Prototype phases).
- **Adapt** and make changes based on the reflections and feedback (Test phase).
- **Cycle** through the process, perhaps pivoting to a different solution, refining the existing one, or even revisiting the Problem Statement.

Embrace the cyclical nature of design thinking, understanding that each loop brings you closer to an effective, empathetic solution. Design thinking continues until we collaboratively achieve innovative results that are transformative for the communities we serve.

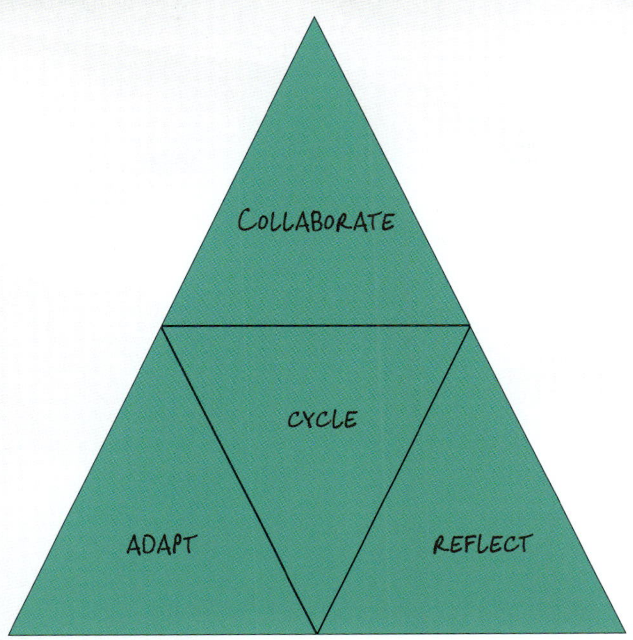

It's Your Turn!

Congratulations! You've achieved a major step in learning about design thinking. This is not the end but the start of a lifelong pursuit of deeper mastery of design thinking with each new project. You can see how this powerful creative problem-solving process works. The students in these chapters made a tangible difference in people's lives, achieving deep satisfaction. It's your turn to step into action.

In our world, progress, social justice, quality of life, and equity often advance one step at a time. One concerned team, one good idea, and one innovative project all contribute to coming closer to these ideals as a society. Collectively, local community actions such as these pave the way for global change, which can happen quickly when critical mass is reached. You have the power to be part of this force of transformation. Become a leader of the changes you want to see in your community and in the world.

Why I Wrote This Book

"I'm just no good at science. Why do we need to learn this anyway?" I heard this far too often from my middle school science students. I wanted—no, *needed*—to shift the limiting attitudes and fixed mindsets of my students and show them that STEM (science, technology, engineering, and mathematics) is fun to learn if you approach it with a sense of inquiry, exploration, and the attitude that mistakes help you learn.

I already used a hands-on approach to science instruction with students running investigations and sharing their findings in our science conversations. This approach worked well for most of my students. But I wanted to reach everyone, especially those who thought that they couldn't learn science. Was there a way to show them *why* the STEM subjects they were learning mattered? Could they learn science by doing science and improving the world at the same time?

Then I met David Kelley and discovered design thinking. David, an inspiring visionary and one of the chief architects of design thinking, brought the design thinking process to the Nueva School, where I taught.

David and Kim Saxe, an extraordinarily talented teacher at Nueva with an engineering background, worked together to create a design lab at the school. Both were mentors to me in learning design thinking. I began using design thinking as a way of teaching science through doing STEM-related design thinking projects. I can still see the faces of my students Sean and Ali when design thinking project-based learning opened up a new world for them—a world where they learned by doing.

Kim and David also started the Design Thinking Institute at Nueva—a summer program gathering creative teachers from around the world to find out how to bring design thinking to their students. They invited me to coach along with them. The institute sparked design thinking projects in many schools, helping teachers learn how to combine project-based learning, community service projects, humanities, and STEM. Sharing my experiences with these teachers was immensely rewarding, and I learned so much from so many of them.

I wondered how I might bring design thinking to people who could not attend a weeklong program or didn't have access to a school design lab. Was there a way to reach students directly? What about a book? My first book, *Teen Innovators: Nine Young People Engineering a Better World with Creative Inventions*, was about students who applied design thinking. I wrote this book to serve as a simple, clear guidebook for students about *learning* design thinking.

In this book, I've distilled what I learned from David and his colleagues at Stanford and IDEO, from Kim and our colleagues at Nueva, and above all, from my students. They inspire this book from start to finish. This book is for you and the next generation of changemakers.

If you find this design thinking guide useful, your journey does not have to end here. Check out my website STEM & Creative Change at https://FredEstes.com/ for further updates, tools, and reading. If you have any feedback, questions, or just want to say hello, please contact me at FredEstesSTEMed@gmail.com. Thank you for your time and interest!

—Fred Estes

Glossary

AFFINITY CLUSTERING: categorizing ideas or data into related groups or clusters, much like organizing research notes under thematic headers for a clearer understanding of a topic

AUGMENTED REALITY (AR): an enhanced version of real-world surroundings created by overlaying them with digital content or information—for example, a phone app that shows star names when pointed at the night sky

BLUETOOTH COMMUNICATIONS: a technology allowing devices to exchange data wirelessly over short distances—for example, a smartphone using Bluetooth technology to connect to wireless headphones to play music

CEREBRAL PALSY: a group of disorders that affect movement and coordination caused by damage to the developing brain before or at birth, which might cause difficulty in walking, talking, or eating

CONTEXT: the circumstances that form the setting for an event, statement, or idea, and in terms of which we can fully understand it—for example, how the context of the American Civil War includes the social and political issues of the time, such as slavery and states' rights

DESIGN THINKING: a method for solving problems by understanding people's needs, coming up with many ideas, and then testing those ideas to find the best solution

DYNAMICS: the patterns of interaction and behavior within a group or community—for example, the give-and-take in a lively conversation, where each person's words, tone, and body language affect everyone else

EMPATHY: seeing the world through someone else's eyes, sensing their emotions, and connecting with their experiences; often used interchangeably with terms such as *sympathy* and *compassion* but different, with *sympathy* meaning feeling sorry for someone else's misfortune and *compassion* meaning to be aware of another's distress with a desire to alleviate it

EQUITY/EQUITABLE: fairness (giving everyone what they need to be successful) but a little different from equality (treating everyone the same); for example, installing ramps in addition to stairs outside buildings helps ensure everyone, including those with mobility issues, can access the building

GROUPTHINK: when a group values harmony over critical analysis, similar to a team unanimously agreeing on an easy project idea to avoid conflict but overlooking potentially innovative but challenging alternatives

HIGH-RESOLUTION: more refined prototypes created from materials that are sturdier and harder to modify, such as wood, PVC, and metal—for example, a sculptor making many sketches on paper and models from clay before carving a piece of marble

HUMIDIFYING DIFFUSER: a device that moisturizes the air and disperses essential oils to provide a pleasant, relaxing atmosphere in a room

IDEATION: a stage in design thinking involving brainstorming, affinity clustering, and selecting among generated ideas; a group brainstorming ideas for a project, categorizing them on sticky notes, and choosing the most promising ones to explore

IMMERSION: in design thinking, to deeply involve oneself in something—for example, when a design thinking team immerses themselves by shadowing someone at their job or taking part in daily activities of a community partner to get a real feel for their challenges and needs

INCUBATOR: a special enclosed crib that helps newborns, especially those with low birth weight, maintain a stable environment with controlled temperature and humidity, supports their growth, and protects them from infections and sensory overload until they are strong enough to thrive outside the incubator

INFORMED CONSENT: getting permission after ensuring someone understands the risks and benefits—for example, a doctor explaining a surgery's pros and cons before a patient agrees to it

ITERATION: refining ideas based on feedback and doing them again, only better

LOW-RESOLUTION: early-stage prototypes made from materials that are easy to work with and change, such as cardboard and foam, to allow for quick adjustments based on feedback—for example, a sculptor sketching ideas on paper with pencil before starting to carve marble

MICRO:BITS: a pocket-sized computer that helps people learn programming and digital skills that has a miniature computer board with lights and buttons and is often used in school projects

MICROCONTROLLER: a chip designed to manage specific operations in an electronic device; the "brain" of everyday gadgets such as a digital camera or a microwave oven

MICROELECTRONICS: very small electronic components, often built at a microscopic scale, such as the technology that makes your smartphone work

MINDSET: based on Carol Dweck's mindset concept that individuals possess either a fixed mindset, with static and unchangeable abilities, or a growth mindset, with abilities developed through effort and learning that can lead to greater success and overall well-being, as it fosters resilience, a love of learning, and a willingness to embrace challenges

MINIMUM VIABLE PRODUCT: the simplest form of a new product that allows community partners to use it, with just the essential features to satisfy early adopters—for example, a basic version of an app to see if people like the concept before making a more complete version

MODEL: a representation of a system or thing, often smaller in scale, that helps designers understand and communicate all or part of their ideas, such as when architects make small versions of a building to test ideas and get reactions

NOTICE: encouraging designers to be self-aware; recognize their values, biases, and assumptions to help them design with empathy; and ensure they meet genuine needs instead of imposing their own ideas—for example, how drawing attention to the lack of diverse representation in movies and TV shows led to calls for more inclusive casting and storylines

OUTLIER: an idea that deviates from the norm, such as proposing a unique project topic that challenges conventional viewpoints in a group discussion

PERSONA: in design thinking, a fictional character that represents a specific group of community partners or stakeholders to help designers understand and address the genuine needs and behaviors of their audience, such as Tech-Savvy Tina to represent people who always have the latest tech gear

PHASE-CHANGING MATERIAL: a material that absorbs or releases heat as it changes phases (for example, from solid to liquid or liquid to gas); used by designers in a variety of applications, such as thermal energy storage and temperature regulation and in some types of ice packs and clothing to keep people cool or warm

PIVOT: a significant shift in strategy or approach, such as how Team Syphon pivoted when they switched from the humidifying diffuser idea to the sensor strategy

PRIVILEGE: in the context of social justice, the unearned advantages or rights that a person receives because of their identity or background, such as when some elite colleges grant automatic admission to a certain number of the children of wealthy or famous alumni

PROTOTYPE: an early model of something, such as a new machine or product used to test ideas and make improvements; to prototype processes or software

REFLECT: a continual process of assessing principles throughout the design phase; a collaborative evaluation of goals and outcomes by designers and community partners to ensure continual learning and a commitment to equity, inclusivity, and global awareness; for example, after designing a community center, the meetings' designers and residents frequently have to evaluate its accessibility and inclusivity, making necessary modifications to better serve all community members

SENSOR: in microelectronics, a device that detects changes in the environment and sends data to a control device—for example, when a thermostat senses temperature changes and adjusts the heat or air conditioning

SOCIAL JUSTICE: the idea that everyone deserves equal rights and opportunities and that the goal is to treat all people fairly, no matter who they are or where they come from

STAKEHOLDER: an individual or group that has an interest in a project or decision—for example, students, teachers, parents, and neighbors involved in a school building project

SUMP PUMP: a pump that turns on automatically when the water reaches a certain level and removes the water from a low spot in a building, such as a basement

SUSTAINABLE/SUSTAINABILITY: refers to practices and methods that meet our current environmental, social, and economic needs without damaging the ability of future generations to meet their own. It involves using resources in a way that preserves the planet, supports equitable social systems, and ensures long-term ecological health and well-being.

SYNTHESIS: combining different ideas or pieces of information to form a single, clear idea or solution, such as blending two or more songs together to create a mash-up, a synthesis of different tunes to produce a new, unique sound

SYSTEMIC: something that affects a large group or system, such as a body, economy, or society—for example, a systemic societal condition, when persistent patterns of poverty span generations and are perpetuated by structural factors such as lack of access to quality education or health care

THEME: in design thinking, a main idea or subject that emerges from examining data or stories that helps in understanding users' needs and perspectives—for example, if some college students are working with the Office of Student Life on improving the student experience and hear about end-of-semester difficulties, including loss of sleep, worry, relationship troubles, and problems focusing on schoolwork, in several interviews and focus groups, which the team might then identify as a theme of "stress and anxiety around exam time"

TRACHEOTOMY TUBE: a tube that is inserted into the trachea (windpipe) to help a person breathe; used when a person cannot breathe on their own because of a blockage or injury to the airway; often used with a ventilator in a hospital

TRADE-OFF: in engineering, when increasing one factor results in decreasing another—for example, increasing the size of a phone's battery so it will last longer but knowing it will make the phone heavier

VIRTUAL REALITY (VR): a simulated experience that can be similar to or entirely different from the real world; an experience that immerses users in a digital environment, such as wearing goggles to explore a virtual jungle or the inside of a molecule

Source Notes

6 "Many people say . . . make a difference.": Gitanjali Rao, personal interview with the author via web conferencing, April 16, 2020.

6–7 "We think we're . . . on the street.": Javier, quoted in "Project Invent—A Team's Journey," YouTube video, posted by Project Invent, February 27, 2018, https://www.youtube.com/watch?v=Gk-kUnnjunY, 0:36.

7 "Blindness is such . . . to the project.": Project Invent Team Syphon, personal interview with the author via web conferencing, October 4, 2022.

8 "I didn't know . . . was super humbling.": Project Invent Team Syphon, personal interview.

10 "Wow, [they] really . . . to help us.": Project Invent Team Syphon, personal interview.

19 "Knowing yourself is . . . of all wisdom.": John Bartlett and Justin Kaplan, *Bartlett's Familiar Quotations*, 17th ed. (Boston: Little, Brown, 2002), 395.

19 "First seek to . . . to be understood.": Stephen R. Covey, *The 7 Habits of Highly Effective People: Powerful Lessons in Personal Change* (New York: Free Press, 1989), 53.

36 "Empathy is about . . . person in yourself.": Cressida Leyshon, "This Week in Fiction: Mohsin Hamid," *New Yorker*, September 16, 2012, https://www.newyorker.com/books/page-turner/this-week-in-fiction-mohsin-hamid.

36 "You can observe . . . by just watching.": Yogi Berra Quotes," BrainyQuote, accessed March 8, 2024, https://www.brainyquote.com/quotes/yogi_berra_125285.

44 "How many hours . . . I'm barely awake.": Project Invent Team Syphon, personal interview.

74 "If the ladder . . . wrong place faster.": Covey, *7 Habits*, 76.

90 "If you always . . . you always got.": "Quote by Henry Ford," Goodreads, accessed March 10, 2024, https://www.goodreads.com/quotes/904186-if-you-always-do-what-you-ve-always-done-you-ll-always.

90 "It is easier . . . a new one.": LABOV, "I Have an Idea," LABOV, April 12, 2021, https://www.labov.com/i-have-an-idea.

103 "At first, during . . . our best idea.": Project Invent Team Syphon, personal interview.

109 "We would all . . . make it better.' ": Project Invent Team Syphon, personal interview.

110 "Never doubt that . . . that ever has.": Donald Keys, *Earth at Omega: Passage to Planetization* (Boston: Branden, 1982), 79.

112 "Occasionally, the designers . . . principle,' Yurchenco says.": Kyle Vanhemert, "The Engineer of the Original Apple Mouse Talks About His Remarkable Career," *Wired*, August 18, 2014, https://www.wired.com/2014/08/the-engineer-of-the-original-apple-mouse-talks-about-his-remarkable-career.

128 "Before I discovered . . . of poor farmers.": William Kamkwamba, "How I Harnessed the Wind," video, TED, July 2009, https://www.ted.com/talks/william_kamkwamba_how_i_harnessed_the_wind?language=en, 1:18.

128 "Now I go even bigger. Superpower!": William Kamkwamba and Bryan Mealer, *The Boy Who Harnessed the Wind: A True Story of Survival* (New York: Puffin, 2015), 175.

132 "We went to . . . figure it out.": Lilli, Project Invent Team Squggle, personal interview with the author via web conferencing, October 7, 2022.

149 "If we do . . . done it before.": Joshua Davis, *Spare Parts: Four Undocumented Teenagers, One Ugly Robot, and the Battle for the American Dream* (New York: Farrar, Straus and Giroux, 2014), 112.

150 "A mind once . . . its old dimensions.": quoteresearch, "Quote Origin: Every Now and Then a Man's Mind Is Stretched by a New Idea or Sensation, and Never Shrinks Back to Its Former Dimensions," Quote Investigator, March 29, 2023, https://quoteinvestigator.com/2023/03/29/stretch.

150 "It always seems . . . it is done.": quoteresearch, "It Always Seems Impossible Until It's Done," Quote Investigator, January 5, 2016, https://quoteinvestigator.com/2016/01/05/done.

150 "The people who . . . ones who do.": Joe Jachim, "25 Steve Jobs Quotes That Will Inspire You to 'Think Different,'" *hello innovation* (blog), accessed October 15, 2023, https://www.helloinnovation.com/blog/25-steve-jobs-quotes.

153 "almost like a . . . who are blind.": "Project Invent," 1:33.

153 "Personally, I've learned . . . be aware of.": "Project Invent," 2:50.

154 "I've always wanted . . . into traffic anymore.": "Project Invent," 3:08.

Selected Bibliography

Bromley, Camille. "How to Use AI to Talk to Whales—and Save Life on Earth." *Wired*, August 29, 2023. https://www.wired.com/story/use-ai-talk-to-whales-save-life-on-earth/.

Clear, James. "Why Trying to Be Perfect Won't Help You Achieve Your Goals (and What Will)." jamesclear.com. Accessed August 30, 2023. https://jamesclear.com/repetitions.

David, Josh. *Spare Parts: Four Undocumented Teenagers, One Ugly Robot, and the Battle for the American Dream*. New York: Crown, 2014.

Estes, Fred. *Teen Innovators: Nine Young People Engineering a Better World with Creative Inventions*. Minneapolis: Zest Books, 2022.

Gibbons, Sarah. "User Needs Statements: The 'Define' in Design Thinking." nngroup.com, March 24, 2019. https://www.nngroup.com/articles/user-need-statements.

Gray, C. M., and K. Brown. "Equity-Centered Design Thinking in Higher Education: A Framework for Social Justice in Learning and Teaching." *Change: The Magazine of Higher Learning* 50, no. 3 (2018): 16–23.

Gray, Dave, Sunni Brown, and James Macanufo. *Gamestorming: A Playbook for Innovators, Rulebreakers, and Changemakers.* 1st ed. Sebastopol, CA: O'Reilly, 2010.

Harmon, Jeanine. "Design Thinking Meets a Community Action Project." Edutopia, August 22, 2013. https://www.edutopia.org/blog/design-thinking-community-action-project-jeanine-harmon.

IDEO. *The Field Guide to Human-Centered Design*. San Francisco: IDEO, 2015.

Joachim, Joe. "25 Steve Jobs Quotes That Will Inspire You to 'Think Different.'" helloinnovation.com. Accessed October 15, 2023. https://www.helloinnovation.com/blog/25-steve-jobs-quotes.

Kamkwamba, William. "How I Harnessed the Wind." TED, July 2009. https://www.ted.com/talks/william_kamkwamba_how_i_harnessed_the_wind?language=en.

Kamkwamba, William, and Bryan Mealer. *The Boy Who Harnessed the Wind: A True Story of Survival.* New York: Puffin, 2016.

Lockwood, Thomas, and Edgar Papke. *Innovation by Design: How Any Organization Can Leverage Design Thinking to Produce Change, Drive New Ideas, and Deliver Meaningful Solutions.* Newbury, MA: Redwheel/Weiser, 2018.

Patterson, Kerry, Joseph Grenny, Ron McMillan, and Al Switzler. *Crucial Conversations: Tools for Talking When Stakes Are High.* New York: McGraw Hill, 2002.

Pinedo, David. "An Introduction to Liberatory Design." UX Collective, July 20, 2020. https://uxdesign.cc/an-introduction-to-liberatory-design-9f5d3fe69ff9.

"Project Invent—A Team's Journey." YouTube video, 3:52. Posted by Project Invent, February 27, 2018. https://www.youtube.com/watch?v=Gk-kUnnjunY.

Von Oech, Roger. *A Whack on the Side of the Head.* New York: Grand Central, 2008.

Going Further

Articles

Busche, Laura. "The Skeptic's Guide to Low-Fidelity Prototyping." Smashing Magazine, October 6, 2014. https://www.smashingmagazine.com/2014/10/the-skeptics-guide-to-low-fidelity-prototyping/.
This article provides a comprehensive look at low-fidelity prototyping and its value in the design thinking process.

Books

Brown, Tim. *Change by Design*. New York: HarperBusiness, 2019.
This book by the CEO of IDEO offers an insightful look into design thinking, with detailed explanations of each phase.

Burnett, Bill, and Dave Evans. *Designing Your Life: How to Build a Well-Lived, Joyful Life*. 1st ed. New York: Alfred A. Knopf, 2016.
Burnett and Evans of the Stanford d.school show how to apply the principles of design thinking to your personal life.

Doeden, Matt. *Conflict Resolution: How to Communicate, Negotiate, Compromise, and More*. Minneapolis, Twenty-First Century Books, 2012.
Doeden explains how to understand the roots of conflict, open lines of communication, and come up with solutions that work for many people.

Dweck, Carol S. *Mindset: The New Psychology of Success*. New York: Ballantine Books, 2006.
This ground-breaking book presented the concept of mindset to the general public, summarizing over thirty years of her academic research.

Kelley, Tom, and David Kelley. *Creative Confidence: Unleashing the Creative Potential within Us All*. New York: Crown Business, 2013.
From the founders of IDEO, this book offers insights into fostering creativity, with a focus on building empathy.

Knapp, Jake. *Sprint: How to Solve Big Problems and Test New Ideas in Just Five Days*. New York: Simon and Schuster, 2016.
This book provides a detailed five-day process for solving tough problems, focusing mainly on testing ideas.

Lewrick, Michael, Patrick Link, and Larry Leifer. *The Design Thinking Playbook*. Hoboken, NJ: John Wiley & Sons, 2018.
This comprehensive guide covers each stage of design thinking with practical examples.

Svoboda, Elizabeth. *The Life Heroic: How to Unleash Your Most Amazing Self.* Minneapolis: Zest Books, 2019.
This well-researched book is packed with stories of teens who have started organizations to help people, save lives, and perform everyday acts of heroism.

Zaki Warfel, Todd. *Prototyping: A Practitioner's Guide*. Brooklyn: Rosenfeld Media, 2009.
This guide offers a deep dive into prototyping techniques, tools, and best practices, including case studies.

Digital Tools

Evernote
https://evernote.com/free
Besides being a powerful note-taking app, Evernote can also digitize and organize your sticky notes. Just take a photo within the app, and it can recognize the text, making it easy to search for specific notes later. Start with the free version, and then upgrade as needed.

Google Lens
https://lens.google/
While not specifically designed for sticky notes, Google Lens can capture written text in images. Point your camera at the text, and Google Lens can copy it for you to paste into a document or send in a message. Google Lens is built into the Chrome browser.

Microsoft OneNote
https://www.microsoft.com/en-us/microsoft-365/onenote/digital-note-taking-app
With its Microsoft Office Lens feature, you can take pictures of your sticky notes, and OneNote will automatically crop and enhance the images. The app can also recognize and transcribe text from the images. MS OneNote comes free with your paid subscription to the Microsoft 365 suite.

Mural
https://www.mural.co/
This digital whiteboard allows teams to collaborate, both in-person and remotely. It is easy to learn, and there is a free version.

Notion

https://www.notion.so/product

Notion is primarily a productivity tool, known for its versatility, customizability, and collaboration features. There is a template for organizing sticky notes. Notion is more comprehensive than Evernote or OneNote, but it takes more time to learn because of all that it can do.

Post-it

https://www.post-it.com/3M/en_US/post-it/ideas/app/faq/

This app lets you capture multiple sticky notes at once, organize them on digital boards, and share with others. It can even transcribe the text on the notes, making them searchable.

The Stoke Deck

https://stokedeck.io/

Created by a student at the Stanford d.school, this app lets you generate warm-up ideas one at a time.

StormBoard

https://stormboard.com/

This is another easy-to-use digital whiteboard with a free version. They are also making an AI add-in.

Online Courses

Coursera: Introduction to Design Thinking

https://www.coursera.org/lecture/uva-darden-design-thinking-innovation/introduction-to-design-thinking-IvE41

Many universities offer design thinking courses on Coursera, which typically includes a deep dive into the Define phase. This is a comprehensive place to start at no cost.

Stanford d.school: Design Thinking Bootleg

https://dschool.stanford.edu/resources/design-thinking-bootleg

This set of tools and methods from the d.school at Stanford is available as a free PDF. It includes exercises and methods to practice building empathy.

Stanford d.school: Virtual Crash Course in Design Thinking

https://www.youtube.com/watch?v=pmjyZPibH14

Stanford's d.school provides a free, ninety-minute video and set of resources.

Websites

MB Collaborative: "Six Creative Warmups to Get Your Team in the Right Mindset"
https://mbcollab.com/blog/six-creative-warmups-to-get-your-team-in-the-right-mindset
These are great ways to get your meeting started and off to a creative start.

National Equity Project
https://www.nationalequityproject.org/
The National Equity Project is dedicated to empowering individuals and fostering the growth of self-reliant, knowledgeable, and equitable communities through leadership and systemic transformation. They aim to reshape the life experiences, prospects, and choices available to children and families that have traditionally been underserved by our societal structures and institutions.

Project Invent
https://projectinvent.org/
Project Invent's goal is to empower students with the twenty-first-century skills to succeed and make global impacts through invention, and to create a generation of fearless, compassionate problem solvers.

Stanford d.school: Prototyping Dashboard
https://dschool.stanford.edu/resources/prototyping-dashboard
This concise resource has best practices and tips on the Prototype phase of the design thinking process.

Index

Acknowledgments

Writing this book has been an incredible journey of discovery and growth, and I could not have completed it without the support and encouragement of many wonderful and exceptionally skilled people. I have learned so much from you all.

I am deeply grateful to the following:

- The Project Invent students and teachers interviewed and consulted, as well as my students at the Nueva School, who inspired me to write this book in the first place. Thanks to curious students everywhere who invent and work to make this world a better place.
- All the wonderful, dedicated people at Project Invent, including Connie Liu, founder and Nueva School colleague; Jax Chaudhry, the inspiring CEO; Autumn Hamra, who is unfailingly helpful; and Leigh Monistere, who coordinated the interviews and is now pursuing graduate study.
- My colleagues and mentors at the Nueva School and the Stanford d.school and IDEO.
- My extraordinary agent, Andy Ross, who championed this book.
- All the talented professionals at Lerner Publishing Group, including my editors Shaina Olmanson, Lauren Foley, Casey Barber, and Delores Barton; the design team, including Danielle Carnito, Athena Currier, and Martha Kranes; photo researcher Giliane Mansfeldt; Megan Ciskowski and the marketing team; and Hallie Warshaw, now an independent, self-described "Digital Nomad."
- Daphne Gray-Grant for unfailing moral support and great writing advice.
- Macy Decker, our town librarian for many years, who let me in early and let me stay late, and librarians everywhere encouraging literacy and defending our right to read.
- My seventh-grade English teacher, Donna Ryan, who encouraged me to keep writing and to edit more.
- My friends Ron and Dan for their consistent support and encouragement, always.
- Mom and Dad for nurturing my love of books and for letting me read for hours at a time.
- My daughter, Laurel, for her insights on design, and our friend Laura for interesting math diversions and science news.
- My wife, Heather, for her patience, support, and understanding throughout the life of this book project, as well as for reading endless drafts with a keen eye for logical narrative and a poet's ear for language.

To everyone who has been a part of this journey, thank you most sincerely. This book would not have been possible without you.

About the Author

Fred Estes is an educator and the author of *Teen Innovators: Nine Young People Engineering a Better World with Creative Inventions.* For nearly two decades, he taught science in a school near his home in San Francisco. Before that he taught high school English, worked as a financial analyst, joined an AI start-up, developed corporate training programs, and earned a doctorate in education. Currently, he teaches graduate students and teachers about design thinking, research methods, innovation, creative teaching methods, and hands-on STEM curriculum. He enjoys reading science and science fiction; writing about design thinking, new ideas, and STEM; and—best of all—working with students on design projects. If you want to share an idea, ask a question, or make a comment, write him at FredEstesSTEMed@gmail.com, and he will answer. He also says that a major contribution of science is the discovery that dark chocolate contains healthy antioxidants.

Photo Acknowledgments

Image credits: Courtesy of Project Invent, pp. 7, 16, 44, 103, 120, 137 all; SolStock/Getty Images, p. 33; (c) UNICEF/UN0678687Aleksey Filippov, p. 72; AzmanJaka/Getty Images, p. 78; Maskot/Getty Images, p. 87; unaihuiziphotography/Getty Images, p. 94; Ian Hubball/Alamy, p. 95; andresr/Getty Images, p. 98; SeDmi/Shutterstock, p. 124 (top); Sawat Banyenngam /Shutterstock, p. 124 (middle); Anton Starikov/Shutterstock, p. 124 (bottom); Erik (HASH) Hersman/Wikimedia Commons (CC BY 2.0), p. 129; Xinhua/Alamy, p. 139; Design Elements: Anastasiia Gevko/ Shutterstock; Mega Pixel/Shutterstock; Marjan Blan/Unsplash; mustafa bashari/Unsplash.

Cover: mrnvb/Shutterstock; Elnur/Shutterstock; Logo Mimi/Shutterstock; Anastasiia Gevko/Shutterstock; Mega Pixel/Shutterstock.